Townsend's Folding Globe

Mythos Press

Map reproduction courtesy of the Norman B. Leventhal Map & Education
Center at the Boston Public Library

Townsend's Folding Globe

A WORLD IN LETTERS FROM GOLD RUSH CALIFORNIA
BY DENNIS TOWNSEND, EDUCATOR AND INVENTOR

Edited and Annotated by Elaine Zorbas

Foreword
by
James H. Nottage

MYTHOS
PRESS

2022

Townsend's Folding Globe

A world in letters from Gold Rush California
by Dennis Townsend, educator and inventor

Copyright © 2022 by Elaine Zorbas

First edition
First printing

ISBN-13: 978-0-9889314-4-2

Published by Mythos Press
Post Office Box 566
Plymouth, California 95669

Cover by: D. Zorbas
Map reproduction courtesy of the Norman B. Leventhal Map & Education Center at the Boston
Public Library

Printed in the United States of America

CONTENTS

List of Illustrations

Foreword

The United States was on the move in 1852. War with Mexico concluded in 1848, gaining what politicians, journalists, and the public claimed as the country's "Manifest Destiny," a vibrant and ambitious nation stretching from the Atlantic to the Pacific. The lure of gold discovered at Sutter's Mill, the beckoning of "free" land in Oregon, and creation of a Mormon homeland in Utah, all tempted thousands to journey west. The year 1852 marked the largest westward trail migration prior to the Civil War. As one historian points out, it was a number equal to two times the population of Chicago at the time—some 70,000 people, 50,000 of whom were headed for California itself.

By this time, the route westward was generally well-known and the experiences of those who had made the journey were filtering back to the East in personal letters, newspaper accounts, and a growing number of official reports and narrative books. In December of 1852, a pictorial expression of the experience, "Jones's Great Pantoscope of California, The Rocky Mountains, Salt Lake City, Nebraska & Kansas," premiered at Boston's Amory Hall. This narrative of the California-Oregon trail west was a giant, moving, painted screen, based, according to its promoter, upon over 1,500 daguerreotypes photographed along the way over the previous two years. Enthusiastic crowds paid for the entertainment value of imagining the way west. Some who were courageous enough were thus motivated to find their way toward dreamed of golden riches.

Earlier this same year, a young Vermont school teacher named Dennis Townsend was swept west with the crowd and along with his young wife moved by wagon to California. They were one small part of this record migration headed to that destination, facing the specter of cholera and other real and imagined challenges and threats. While the stories of other travelers are recorded in diaries, letters, and reminiscences, many of these have been lost in fading memories and with the ravages of time. Fortunately, unheralded or unknown accounts are still being revealed, expanding our knowledge and appreciation for the times and experiences of the people. Such is the case of the Townsend narrative.

Townsend, a teacher, was a gifted and dedicated writer who sent a large volume of descriptive letters to members of his family in the East, briefly narrating the trip and sharing more details of the life he lived in California thereafter. Preserved in public institutions and discovered by historian Elaine Zorbas, the letters are now shared with us, along with details about the lives of the writer and his family. The editor gives the letters context and greater meaning through informative introductions and annotations. Zorbas is uniquely qualified to share the Townsend story. Two of her previous books, Fiddletown: From Gold Rush to Rediscovery, and Banished & Embraced: The Chinese in Fiddletown and the Mother Lode, provide much detail for the rich history of the community in which Townsend first settled. With Zorbas' present volume, Townsend's Folding Globe, however, there is content going beyond the local or personal. From the vantage point of Townsend's experiences, this too is a "pantoscope" or panorama, of lives played out following the overland journey.

Dennis Townsend fulfilled many different roles during his life: hopeful gold miner, teacher, school superintendent, daguerreotypist, musician, businessman, postman, father, husband, and intriguingly an inventor. His is a rich story, but one with an unexpected and tragic conclusion. Through his own words and those of his editor, you are invited on a personal journey through a fascinating man's life. These are the everyday stories of a well-educated individual, documenting the beginnings and growth of the gold-rush era California communities of Fiddletown and Volcano. These are personal stories that are staged in the context of local, community, and even national history.

Just as Dennis Townsend's letters helped to dissolve the distance between his immediate family and those living in the East, they help to shorten the distance between ourselves and nineteenth century California. It is a narrative of personal triumph and angst. Just as importantly, it is an odyssey of gold rush era community struggles with crime, the advancement of commerce and institutions, and the complexities of growth under the blessings and challenges of an ethnically diverse population.

We can celebrate the survival of the Townsend letters, some of which surely traveled by ship around the horn to the East coast, many that likely moved to their destination by wagon and coach, and a few, after completion of the transcontinental railroad, that went with speed by mail coach on rails. It is the skill with which editor Elaine Zorbas has made them available that completes the journey. Her accomplishment is no less notable than Dennis Townsend's inspired invention of a folding world globe, created for teachers, that was transformed from flat pieces of printed paper to the full roundness of the earth.

James H. Nottage

Chief Curator Emeritus
Eiteljorg Museum of American Indians and Western Art

Preface

The correspondence of Vermonter Dennis Townsend entered my life after Paul Carnahan, Librarian of the Vermont Historical Society (VHS), wrote a letter in June 2004 to the Fiddletown Preservation Society, relating the existence of Townsend's letters along with an 1857 photograph of Fiddletown. The information came my way, since I had written about Dennis Townsend in my book on the history of Fiddletown, a town established during the Gold Rush in the Sierra Nevada foothills southeast of Sacramento. Dennis served as the community's first Postmaster, its first schoolteacher, and the Amador County School Superintendent. He was the inventor of a collapsible globe of the world for teaching geography, as well as a person of many talents. As there are very few sources with first-person accounts of early life in Fiddletown, these letters are of great interest.

For the purposes of this book, I chose to reproduce 29 of the letters written by Dennis Townsend between 1852 and 1868—27 written from the mining towns of Fiddletown and Volcano in California, and the final two from his family home in Felchville, Vermont. Dennis started writing letters to his family in 1835 when he was an 18 year-old student. His later letters, composed in the most creative part of his life, are historically significant in depicting the early settlement of these two gold rush boom towns, his role in their development, and the impact of local, state and national events in the 1850s and 1860s. Dennis provided perspective on Rancheria Massacre in Amador County, the Know Nothing Party and the effects of the Civil War on both his family and the community. His letters from St. Joseph, Missouri and a long letter describing the overland journey add his impressions to the voluminous letters and journals recounting personal recollections of migration to California following the discovery of gold.

Dennis was one of fifteen children. His correspondence with members of his family occurred during a period of the nation's growth, when developments in transportation and communication by mail and telegraph collapsed time and distance. At the same time, reforms in public education accompanied the nationwide expansion of common schools. Dennis' letters reflect some of these changes, also encapsulating the abiding and deep connections between family members as they spread across the states. His town of origin, Reading, Vermont, and Fiddletown, California were close in size, though far apart in character. While living in this new, evolving region of California, Dennis compared the rough and violent surroundings of Fiddletown to refined New England society, evaluating whether the perceived benefits of climate, health, and potential prosperity were sufficient reasons for settling permanently in the state.

Most of Dennis' letters and those from several of his siblings reside in manuscript collections at the Vermont Historical Society's Howard & Alba Leahy Library in Barre, Vermont under the heading *William Townsend Family Letters 1827-1899*. As I learned much later, original copies of additional letters are held by the University of Texas at Austin in the Dolph Briscoe Center for American History, under *Dennis Townsend Papers, 1833-1858*.

It has taken me many years to make these letters available in book form. After learning about their existence, I eagerly read all the Dennis Townsend letters spanning 1835-1868 in the VHS Leahy Library collection, initially coming to me as photocopies. I transcribed 16 letters relating to California plus the two letters sent in 1868 from Felchville, Vermont after Townsend returned there to develop his invention. It became a challenge for me to decode Dennis' handwriting, fluctuating between elegant and scrawling depending on his time and his emotions.

In 2011, I realized that I had never examined Dennis' letters from the University of Texas which had been partially itemized by the VHS and were available from them as digital scans. These letters opened up a rich repository that included an account of the Townsend's overland journey, arrival in Volcano, plus seven letters from Fiddletown that intersected in time with those in the VHS collection. I transcribed these letters, still a challenging endeavor, but easier to manipulate in their digital format.

Meanwhile, the Vermont Historical Society had digitalized all letters written by Dennis as well as selected correspondence of his siblings. In 2012, I requested and received digital scans of letters from a few of Dennis' brothers and sisters. Some of letters offered additional information on his activities and yielded another perspective of him. I intended to publish my transcriptions of the letters, but turned away from this project for a few years to research another subject relating to Fiddletown. That pause was auspicious.

Another important source came my way through a member of the Fiddletown Preservation Society—a photocopied typed manuscript written in 1964 by Bessie K. Meacham, *A Chronicle of the Family of William Townsend, 1780-1865 and Susannah Smith 1783-1820 and Hannah G. Bigelow, 1794-1865: The Story of the Comings and Goings of Fifteen*

Sons and Daughters. Bessie Meacham was the granddaughter of one of the Townsend siblings, Francis Torrey Townsend who had written a short autobiography in 1905, prefaced by a family genealogy of his siblings. Meacham obtained and read all of the voluminous family letters, saved by successive generations in the family home in Vermont. That was no small task because there were hundreds of letters. In her chronicle, Meacham incorporated information from the letters to present a chronological account of the various siblings' lives, documenting their simultaneous activities as they matured, worked, moved away from home, married, had families and died. She wrote, "If we trace the history of one family, living in Windsor County, Vermont, members of which eventually lived in states from Vermont to Texas, Massachusetts to California, we shall have in miniature a picture of the 'Great Migration' in American history."

Bessie Meacham understood the value of preserving historical documents, professionally serving as a librarian (my own profession) at LeMoyne College, a historically black college in Memphis, Tennessee. She donated most of the family letters to the Vermont Historical Society. However, recognizing the importance of the letters written by Dennis, she also donated some of his letters along with a few letters of his siblings to the University of Texas at Austin.

A number of Dennis' letters became separated from the VHS collection covering October 1868 to May 1873, except for two letters written from Vermont in December 1868 and included in this collection. These letters cover his time away in Vermont where he stayed with his family to produce and promote his invention. Fortunately, Bessie Meacham created index cards for each sibling with details and quotes from their letters. I obtained copies of the Index pertaining to Dennis Townsend from the VHS and have extensively used information from them to give a more complete view of his life.

The Vermont Historical Society Leahy Library developed a finding aid that describes the William Townsend collection, summarizing the scope and content of each sibling's letters, *William Townsend Family Letters, 1827-1899, MSC 133* (Barre:Vermont, 2004, rev. 2020). It is available as a PDF document, https://vermonthistory.org/documents/findaid/townsend.pdf. I consulted this source for insight into the various family members. Meacham's *Chronicle* and Index are referenced throughout.

Characteristics of the letters

Printed letters in a book, while legible, cannot convey the qualities of handwritten letters. Dennis chose his words carefully, often striking a word out and substituting a more felicitous word or phrase. For ease of reading, I have not included the strikeouts, but do refer to the appearance of handwriting changes within individual letters. In some letters, the page was covered with additional notes inserted at the top, bottom and in the margins, as described in footnotes. Other pages were difficult to decipher. With the few misspellings that occurred, I added the corrected word in brackets [ ], which are also used for any of my clarifications. The word "inclosed" used at that time was changed to "enclosed." I occasionally inserted commas for clarity, but otherwise no changes in punctuation were needed. Dennis underlined words for emphasis, replicated in the book as used by him.

One of the most important letters, written from Volcano in January 23, 1853, is also the most puzzling. The handwriting of this letter, which describes the overland journey, differs from all the other letters written by Dennis. Yet in tone and the rephrasing of words, the style is consistent with his other letters. I give samples of handwriting from this letter, also discussed in Chapter 2 and in the letter's footnote.

Dennis wrote six letters in 1853, but later correspondence became intermittent, especially after he became a busy postmaster and teacher. His letters often summarized what had changed in his life. A few letters conveyed similar information when Dennis wrote to more than one member of the family simultaneously. Many letters are elliptical, leaving out details about his surroundings. My commentary aims to point out the gaps and to fill in additional information, providing context and background.

Dennis' letters focused on himself and not on his immediate family. Upon his marriage, he referred to his wife, Lizzy, conveying his pride in her abilities. Afterwards, he only gave passing reference to her and their children. When Lizzy's sisters joined them in California, he did not reveal their first names, only providing the customary married surname. The roles of Dennis and Lizzy were conventional for their period with the husband acting as primary breadwinner while the wife cared for the home and children. Lizzy corresponded with some of Dennis' sisters and no doubt the grueling work in those days of maintaining a household kept her from exploring her abilities.

Dennis was an articulate and thoughtful correspondent whose character shines forth in his letters—earnest, loyal, hard-working, fair-minded, morally upright, compassionate, and deeply devoted to his Vermont family—always striving to improve himself economically and morally. He was pious and humble rather than dogmatic, resigned to fate, yet determined to be optimistic despite a morose disposition. Poor health, with recurrent illness, affected him physically and mentally, ultimately shortening his life. The struggle to prosper and survive is part of his story.

The content of this book extends beyond the Dennis Townsend letters to encompass his life from beginning to the end, with education being a key component. The first chapter introduces his family and the influences that governed his development, tracing his path from student in New England to teaching school in other states. The last two chapters cover the period in Vermont where he devised his invention, followed by his return to live in Fiddletown, California where he spent his last years.

Note that footnotes are renumbered in each chapter and group of letters.

The source of each letter written by Dennis Townsend is indicated at the bottom:

VHS MSC 133:7 for Vermont Historical Society

UTAustin/VHS MSC 133:8 for University of Texas at Austin's copies, digitally available at VHS.

Letters found in manuscript collections are cited by the name of the writer, the name and place (where known) of the recipient and date: *Townsend, Dennis to Susanna Townsend, Jeffrey, New Hampshire, December 21, 1835, VHS MSC133:7.*

CHAPTER 1

Beginnings: Family Foundation

In the spring of 1852 Dennis Townsend and his wife Lizzy embarked on a journey from their home in Carrollton, Illinois to make the overland crossing to California. By choosing to join the thousands of others migrating during the Gold Rush, the Townsends changed the course of their lives. A Vermonter and a teacher by profession, Dennis had lived and worked in several states before heading to the Far West.

Born May 8, 1817, Dennis grew up in the town of Reading, Vermont. His father, William Townsend, of English extraction, moved to Reading as a boy from Lynn, Massachusetts where his family lived since 1635. William became a farmer and his marriage with Susannah Smith produced nine children, the eighth being Dennis. Sadly, Susannah died in April, 1820 when Dennis was only three years old. Another son, Adin, was born a year before his mother died.

Soon after the death of his first wife, William married Hannah Gould Bigelow. Taking on his nine children, Hannah gave birth to eight more. Fifteen of the children survived. The youngest, Marquis, was born in 1835 after Dennis turned eighteen years old. All the children found Hannah to be a loving mother who made no distinction between her stepchildren and those she bore. Dennis referred to her in his letters with great affection and respect. He, too, accepted all the siblings as direct blood relatives with the younger ones called the "second crop." This large family sustained Dennis throughout his life. His letters were written to his parents as well as to several of his brothers and sisters. In this family of letter writers, various members relied on correspondence as the means to inform each other of developments and share family news.

Dennis' early letters to his family began in 1835 when he was an 18-year old student, intent on getting an education to better his life. The economic situation of the Townsend family was extremely strained as his father struggled by farming to support such a large family. A move by the parents to a farm in Norwich, Vermont from 1836 to 1857 did not bring about monetary improvement. Elmer, the eldest sibling, became the financial mainstay of the family. Elmer had relocated to Boston, where he worked as bookkeeper for Jonathan Forbush & Company, a leader in the boot and shoe trade. He eventually became a partner and later, formed

1

his own firm. Throughout his life, he did all he could to help his parents survive, as well as giving needed financial aid to his siblings.

As described by descendent Bessie Meacham, "This was a God-fearing family of sturdy integrity.... Most were pillars of the churches, wherever they settled. " The family did not adhere to a particular Protestant denomination, but maintained a strong faith. Music was embedded in the family, pervasive at church and in the home. Their father, William excelled in singing and played both violin and fife. These musical abilities were inherited by the children; several taught singing and had fine voices, including Dennis who also played the violin.[1]

The Townsend family valued giving both the sons and daughters a good educational foundation. Elmer played a major role in encouraging his siblings to attend school and covering their expenses. Common or public schools were well established in Northern states, including Vermont. These schools were locally controlled and offered rudimentary education, with teachers often barely ahead of their students. Academies, a step above, were privately subsidized and offered a higher level of education to older students which included classical studies and subjects such as rhetoric, history, mathematics and various sciences.[2] The girls in the family—Aurelia, Susan, Eliza and Isabelle— attended academies, as well as Dennis and his brother, William.

While going to an academy in Greenfield, Massachusetts in 1835, Dennis studied hard and contemplated his future. Writing to his brother Orson, he considered going to college to "get along in the world," finding something that "fits my disposition best for employment."[3] At the end of that year with Elmer's advice, he transferred to a better academy in Plainfield, New Hampshire. In a letter to his sister Susan, Dennis confessed that he contended with bashfulness as a "great disease and enemy." Nonetheless, if he can "get a decent education and procure my own bread and butter, it is all that I expect and I was going to say, all that I wish for."[4] Dennis wrote to Susan that he taught a term in a school

---

1 Meacham, Bessie, *A Chronicle of the Family of William Townsend, 1780-1865 and Susannah Smith 1783-1820 and Hannah G. Bigelow, 1794-1865: The Story of the Comings and Goings of Fifteen Sons and Daughters*, 1964.

2 Neem, Johann N., *Democracy's Schools: The Rise of Public Education in America* (Baltimore, John Hopkins University Press, 2017), 62-64.

3 Townsend, Dennis to Orson Townsend, Reading Vermont, November 6, 1835, VHS MSC 133: 7.

4 Townsend, Dennis to Susanna Townsend, Jeffrey, New Hampshire, December 21, 1835, VHS MSC 133: 7.

during the winter of 1838 and that "he enjoyed it for the most part." Then he asked "Are you preparing to go West with the rest of us?"[5] At that time, heading West meant going west and south of New England. As the territory of the U.S. expanded with the Louisiana Purchase and other acquisitions, settlers started moving into lands that were occupied by Indians, gradually becoming new states; the southwest and far west were not acquired by the U.S. until the conclusion of the Mexican-American War in February,1848.[6]

When Dennis was 22 years old and living with the family in nearby Norwich, he entered Dartmouth College in August, 1839. Yet his time spent in college was short. By the following spring he dropped out, planning to leave New England to head west. He thought that he "should like teaching, but that, too, at the West or South, but above all to walk in the way of my duty...to benefit my fellow-beings."[7] Dennis did not want to burden Elmer to support him through college, but his abrupt decision to depart was a shock to this generous brother. When Elmer found out Dennis was about to leave, he wrote to their father,

> I could not think he [Dennis] would take such a course without consulting me. If he has not left on rec't [receipt] of this, please say that I wish him to go ahead at Dartmouth and he shall have money as he may want it. Dennis says his bills are about $65. I send enclosed $100 from which I wish you to pay his bills and keep the balance for yourself."[8]

Dennis was also influenced by his other older brothers—the twins Albert and Alfred and especially, his brother, William. These sons eventually left Vermont for other states. Vermont's rocky soil, harsh climate, and economic decline propelled young men to seek opportunities elsewhere. Between 1840 and 1850, it was the slowest-growing state in the nation.[9] The population of Reading followed the same pattern, going from 1,603 residents in 1820 to 1,171 in 1850 with a decline to 953 in 1880. In future letters, Dennis referred to the difficulties of living in his home state.

---

5 Townsend, Dennis to Susan Townsend, Groton, Mass., April 5, 1839. Enclosed with a letter from Eliza Townsend.

6 For $15 million, Mexico ceded most of the territory in the states of New Mexico, Utah, Nevada, Arizona, California, Texas and western Colorado.

7 Meacham, 6.

8 Elmer Townsend to William [father] Townsend, March 25, 1840, VHS MSC 133:3.

9 Morrissey, Charles T., *Vermont: A Bicentennial History* (New York, W.W. Norton & Company, 1981).

William, three years older than Dennis, had left New England and moved to Marietta, Ohio in 1838 to study and teach in a Sabbath school after he had a religious revelation that made preaching his main objective. William encouraged Dennis attend the Marietta Institution where "you will find the course of study about the same as at Dart' [Dartmouth] except one additional studying the German Language...By coming west you will become acquainted with the southern and western disposition."[10] That November, William wrote to Susan, praising Dennis who was currently staying in Marietta, "I have great confidence in him; he is the smartest of the first lot of Townsends, he has a mind of his own, and is determined to act for himself to stand upon his own bottom."[11]

By February 1841, after "knocking about considerably since leaving Vermont, " Dennis established himself near Jackson, Louisiana where he taught school and also studied. His brothers were not far away. Alfred worked in Vicksburg, Mississippi; Albert, who had recovered from alcoholism, stayed in the interior of Mississippi, "thinking of returning north." William currently taught school in Missouri.[12]

In 1842, William and Dennis reunited. Together they started a subscription school in Burlington, Iowa, housed in the basement of the Methodist Church where they also lived. They increased the number of students from seven to 100 and seemingly, the school thrived. However, by the following year they realized that only a few students had paid cash, whereas the rest relied on bartering, causing the school to ultimately fail.[13] Two years later, after another move, Dennis taught school in Liberty Mississippi. William lived about ten miles away in Darlington, Louisiana.

At some point, Dennis returned to Louisiana where ill health brought him down in Clinton. In May, 1845, he informed his sisters Susan and Eliza that he had "experienced diversified fortune since my visit [home] to New England. While in Iowa and through the succeeding year I was blessed in health, but from July last for eight months I suffered extremely and several times was on the verge of the grave..." Health setbacks were to plague Dennis throughout his life, changing his mood from "highly

10   William Townsend to Dennis Townsend, Dartmouth College, Hanover New Hampshire, March 19, 1840. VHS MSC 133: 13.

11   William Townsend to Susan Townsend, Norwich, Vermont, November 22, 1840, VHS MSC 133:13.

12   Dennis Townsend to William S. Townsend, Norwich, VT, February 5, 1841. VHS MSC 133: 7.

13   Meacham, 9-10.

elated by favorable prospects to deep despondency with dire forebodings of the future." His depression was exacerbated by the sudden death of Albert, one of the twins. "We mourn for him as one whose kind and generous qualities preponderated over his failings. I feel as a breach of no small consideration has been made in the family...[14]

Despite these setbacks, Dennis continued to teach in a school that he anticipated would prosper with plans to add a female teacher. He encouraged Susan and Eliza to join him by practicing the piano in order to fill the position of teaching music. He added, "Alfred, William and myself will most likely spend our days in the South so that you cannot be without friends here....There is society here of every character from best to worst. " Dennis mentioned the presence of a Baptist and a Methodist Church that had a flourishing Sabbath school. He made no mention of slavery.

Several months later Dennis confessed to his brother-in-law at the close of the school term that he had been sick for half the time. "At times I get discouraged and out of heart with life. My pen runs in disorder, directed by a mind of chaos from which fly indigested fragments of thoughts."[15] After writing this despondent letter, Dennis must have again drifted to another location, his whereabouts for the next few years not recorded.

Four years passed until his life turned around for the better. Writing to his parents in 1850 from Carrollton, Illinois, Dennis revealed that he had married a year previously. He did not name his wife, but Elizabeth Ray or "Lizzy" obviously brightened his existence. Now 33 years old, he related his struggles and his improved outlook:

> The vicisitudes [vicissitudes] of life have left their mark upon me. A wig covers my baldness and my upper front teeth are false. The world has used me rather roughly. I have suffered much from sickness and have accomplished but little for myself except clearing expenses though this may be attributed in part to my improvidence. I was ever unsettled and ready to pull up stakes and travel until that fortunate era in my life when I took a fair daughter of Illinois to be my help-mate. May 3rd, 1849 was my wedding day. All that I have to say about my lady is that she suits me exactly. Before leaving the South in connection with another young man I learned the Daguerreotype art. Came to Carrollton: took miniatures 3

---

14 Dennis Townsend to Miss Susanna Townsend, Nashua, New Hampshire. May 31, 1845. VHS MSC 133:7

15 Dennis Townsend to Mr. Horace Herrick, Fitzwilliam, New Hampshire, September 28, 1845. VHS MSC 133:7. Mr. Herrick was the husband of Dennis' sister, Aurelia.

or 4 months which I found unprofitable and resumed my old vocation of teaching…I am now on the 1st quarter of the second year of teaching in Carrollton. I have a good school….The "California fever" has taken off a great many from this village and vicinity.[16]

Dennis resisted the lure of California for two more years in which he continued teaching. But the prospect of embarking on the unknown prevailed. In spring of 1852, he and Lizzy uprooted themselves from Illinois and set off for the promise of California. They too had caught the California fever. The letters reproduced here begin with their journey.

---

16 Dennis Townsend to William and Hannah Townsend, March 3, 1850.

THE WILLIAM TOWNSEND FAMILY[1]

William Townsend	September 8, 1780 –	
	December 19, 1865	
Susannah Smith	May 13, 1783 – April 9, 1820	
Children		
	Elmer Townsend	March 2, 1807 – April 13, 1871 Boston, Mass.
	Orson Townsend	May 6, 1808 – August 24, 1865 Reading, Vt.
	Alfred Townsend	Jan. 13, 1810 – March 10, 1871
		Independence, Texas
	Albert Townsend	Jan. 13, 1810 – April 24, 1845 Carthage, Miss.
	Aurelia Herrick	September 30, 1811 – July 5, 1891 Felchville, Vt.
	Susan (Susanna) Fay	March 20, 1813 – October 19, 1879 Felchville, Vt.
	William S. Townsend	October 16, 1814- September 9, 1864
	Dennis Townsend	May 8, 1817 – February 21, 1874 Stockton, CA
	Adin Townsend	April 16, 1819 – June 19, 1823 Reading, Vt.

William Townsend	September 8, 1780 –	
	December 19, 1865	
Hannah G. Bigelow	July 25, 1794 – February 26, 1884	
Children		
	Eliza Townsend	July 27, 1821 – May 20, 1911 Felchville, Vt.
	Frederick Van Alstyne	April 9, 1824 – July 20, 1893 Springfield, Vt.
	Isabelle Waterman	February 26, 1827 – April 2, 1895 Mapleton, Kansas
	Francis Torrey Townsend	March 5, 1829 – August 25, 1907 Clay, Iowa
	Van Buren Townsend	January 4, 1831 – October 30, 1898 Tampa, Florida
	Velette Townsend	April 18, 1832 – December 11, 1903 Worcester, Mass.
	Marquis Townsend	October 23, 1835 – 1922 Conneaut, Ohio

---

[1] Townsend, Francis Torrey. *Autobiography of Francis Torrey Townsend and Genealogy of the Townsends*, reprint, White River, Junction, Vt., Cummings the Printer, 1905. Includes dates and some biographical information.

Figure 1. William Townsend Family: Parents & Children

7

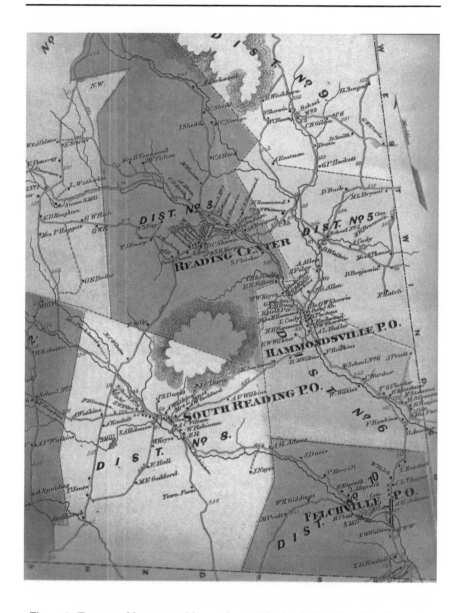

Figure 2. Townsend homestead in northeast District 3, Reading, Vt.: *Courtesy Reading Historical Society*

Figure 3. Lizzie and Dennis Townsend: *Courtesy American Antiquarian Society*

CHAPTER 2

Overland Journey, Arrival in Volcano

The Overland Journey

The first three letters cover the 1852 overland journey to California undertaken by Dennis Townsend and his wife Lizzy—the journey of a lifetime filled with hope and anticipation. That year, the largest migration across the nation occurred. An estimated 50,000 people set forth to start a new life, buoyed by accounts of riches and opportunities ahead in a bountiful land.[1] In contrast to the forty-niners who were mostly men, the emigrants in 1852 included many women and children.

By this time the trails were well established with guidebooks available for prospective travelers. Still, the journey could be treacherous, especially if accidents or illness, such as deadly cholera, created loss and sorrow. The wife and child of a friend of Townsends became ill at the outset. The exposure to changing weather, disease, outdoor living, and unforeseen dangers challenged those making the journey.

Dennis and Lizzy departed with a spirit of adventure in late April embarking on the trip from Carrollton, Illinois to St. Joseph, Missouri, a popular jumping-off point for those coming from Illinois, Indiana and Ohio. Here they purchased provisions for the journey, including feed for their team of oxen. The May 1, 1852 letter from St. Joseph indicates they initially travelled with a company of emigrants from their area of Greene County, Illinois, led by Buck Blackshare.[2] For some reason, they did not remain with that group and there is no description in subsequent letters describing whether or not they travelled with other companions. Emigrants would often share a part of the journey with others going in the same direction. Dennis and Lizzy encountered people whom they knew

---

1 Unruh, John D., Jr. *The Plains Across: The Overland Emigration and the Trans-Mississippi West, 1840-1860* (Urbana, University of Illinois Press, 1979), 120 and chapters 2 and 3, "Public Opinion, 1840-60 and "Motivations and Beginnings." For 1852 accounts, see Merrill J. Mattes, *Platte River Road Narratives* (Chicago, University of Illinois Press, 1988).

2 Oregon-California Trails Association https://www.paper-trail.org/. There is no reference to Blackshare in the extensive database "A Guide to Overland Pioneer Names Documents" or found in local sources by the Greene County Historical and Genealogical Society.

in St. Joseph. Did they travel with any of them along the way? Did they, like most emigrants, outfit a covered wagon pulled by their oxen?

The second letter from Dennis was written on October 5, 1852 after they arrived safely in Volcano, California in the Sierra Nevada foothills after 168 days on the road. He did not describe the journey until several months later in long letter to his entire family written on January 23, 1853. As noted in the footnotes to this letter, the handwriting visibly departs from his usual script. The letter includes personal references to his appearance, the ages of his siblings and their father, and with pride, he introduced Lizzy to his family. The voice is his, and without doubt he authored the letter. He either used a variant handwriting or he dictated the letter to Lizzy.

The trajectory of the Townsend's trip to California followed a well-established route. From the beginning point in St. Joseph, Missouri, Dennis and Lizzy headed north to Ft. Kearny where they embarked upon the Platte River Route, also used for reaching Oregon. This trail took them through the valleys and prairies of what became Nebraska and part of Wyoming. They traversed the Rocky Mountains at the South Pass along the Continental Divide. From there, they veered south to the Salt Lake Cut-off, passing through the verdant Salt Lake valley, and stopping to stay for one week at Salt Lake City. Afterwards, they followed the 300 mile course of the Humboldt River, encountering alkali soil and thick dust as the river narrowed to the Humboldt Sink. The Forty-Mile Desert ahead presented the greatest difficulty for most travelers, but Dennis and Lizzy did not suffer the deprivation of earlier emigrants and their animals. During their journey, trading posts established along this route furnished adequate food and water for humans and livestock. After crossing the desert, they took the cut-off to the Carson River Route leading them along the fertile Carson River valley in present day Nevada to the formidable wall of the eastern Sierra Nevada. The ascension up these steep, rugged granite mountains offered the final challenge for reaching California.

Townsend's account of the overland journey to California covered the major points of the journey with articulate descriptions of changing topography, the beauty of the landscape, the quality of the roads, and dangers along the way, especially illness and crossing rivers. He was particularly eloquent in expressing the transition from the arid land of the desert to the abundance and coolness of the lush Carson Valley. Yet his recap is brief compared to the hundreds of journals diaries, and letters written by others during the Gold Rush and California's early years.

In a single letter, Dennis could not write about the weather changes, hardships and the daily vicissitudes of travelling that are captured in other diaries. Because he wrote this letter to his entire family months after the journey, he may have wanted to give reassurance of their safe arrival by minimizing the travails of the long journey.

Two diaries mentioned here parallel the Dennis Townsend journey in time and the path travelled. They can be consulted for comparison and an expanded version of the trip. Both were written by women and provide more detailed description of the sights along the way to California. They also contain excellent editorial introductions and commentary that delve into the historical background.

Mary Stuart Bailey also hailed from Vermont. At the age of 16, she married Dr. Fred Bailey, ten years older, and moved to Sylvania, Ohio. The Baileys started out on the journey to California from their home on April 13, 1852. Arriving St. Joseph on May 16, they followed the same route as the Townsends. They reached the town of Volcano on October 6, twenty days after Dennis and Lizzy finished their journey. However, like many emigrants the Baileys moved on to Sacramento, where all was unfortunately lost in a destructive fire on November 2.[3]

Lorena Hays made the overland trip one year later than the Townsends. At age 26, she departed for California in 1853 from Barry, Illinois [Pike County] along with her mother, four sisters, and an uncle. Other relatives later joined the party. Lorena avidly wanted to improve her education and had ambitions to be a writer. Arriving in late September 1853, she stayed on in what became Amador County, primarily living in the Ione Valley throughout that decade. Her diary contained evocative descriptions of the landscape as well as her attitudes, thoughts and feelings.[4]

As they passed through lands inhabited by Native American tribes, these diaries and the letters from Dennis describe encounters with Indians. In general, relations between Indians and whites were amicable and peaceful in 1840s through the mid-1850s with mutual interchanges

---

3   Bailey, Mary Stuart, "A Journal of Mary Stuart Bailey, April-October, 1852" in *Ho for California! Women's Overland Diaries from the Huntington Library*, edited and annotated by Sandra L. Myres, (San Marino, Huntington Library, 1980), 49-91. The editor's commentary in "The California Trail, 1850-1859" gives a historical context of the journey. 44-47. The Baileys eventually settled in Santa Cruz in 1858.

4   Watson, Jeanne Hamilton, ed. *To the Land of Gold and Wickedness: The 1848-59 Diary of Lorena L. Hays.* (St. Louis, The Patrice Press, 1988).The editor's introduction to the chapters, "The Trip to California" and "The California Years," traces the journey with step-by-step descriptions of the terrain and excerpts from other emigrant journals.

that included trading goods, providing guidance to trails, and giving aid for those in distress such as lost emigrants and sick Indians.[5] Still, rumors of Indian massacres were rampant, creating fear on the part of emigrants, but largely exaggerated and unsubstantiated.

At the beginning of the journey at the emigrant's camp near St. Joseph, Dennis recounted an interesting occurrence where a conflict with Indians was avoided after a Native American killed an ox belonging to the Blackshare Company. In his letter of May 1, 1852, Dennis expressed skepticism of a tale circulating around in the camp about the revenge killing of three whites by Indians that followed the killing of an Indian. Later in the journey, he referred in the January 23, 1853 letter to encounters with Lakota, Iowa and Pawnee Indians, indicating that their party "escaped unhurt," but providing no details. Although he and Lizzy heard reports from others of "sickness, murder and hair breadth escapes" between Fort Kearny and Fort Laramie, he chose not to pass on the tales to his family. These may well have been stories that contributed to the folklore about Indian savagery.

The Townsends were particularly impressed by the Sioux Indians, "the finest looking Indians we saw on the road," undoubtedly referring to their fine bearing and clothing. The Sioux [of the Plains, known as Lakota] were also subjects of interest for the other travelers. Sioux lived in villages along the Platte River. Mary Stuart Bailey observed on June 22, 1852:

> Passed a Frenchman's blacksmith shop. His wife is a squaw of the Sioux tribe. She sat at the door of their log hut, well drest [dressed], robed in a scarlet blanket. She looked rather sober but well. Another squaw on horse-back chasing a drove of horses & mules, half dressed. We are still on the Platte. Cattle, cattle, it really seems as though the whole country is alive with men, women, horses, mules, cattle & sheep with a smart sprinkling of children."[6]

5 Tate, Michael L., *Indians and Emigrants: Encounters on the Overland Trails* (Norman, University of Oklahoma Press, 2006). See especially 105-143, "Accruing the Benefits," "Responding to the Alarm." Tensions increased in the mid-50s after the passage of so many migrants brought disease and depleted tribal sources of sustenance from bison, wildlife, firewood and grazing lands. See also 156-200, chapter "Emigrant-Indian Interaction."

6 Bailey, 64-65. Squaw, now considered a pejorative term, referred to Indian women. The references by these writers were not written in disrespect but curiosity. For the native people, it must have felt like they were being overrun with emigrants and animals, although on the 25th of June, Mary Bailey described an Indian village having many of their own horses and some cattle, mules and even sheep, 66.

In a diary entry on June 24, 1853, Lorena Hays encountered the Sioux on the move and wrote,

> One day, on the other side of Fort Laramie, we saw a large train of Sioux moving. They fasten their long wigwam poles to their ponies, something as the shafts of a carriage are fastened to horses. Across these, and on the horses' backs are placed all of their baggage and babies, the squaws going before and leading the ponies, while the men ride on horseback without saddles or bridles except a sort they make of buffalo skins without bits. They are, some of them, dressed very fancifully in gay colored blankets and deer skin leggings and moccasins tastefully embroidered with beads and fringe. Some of the men, and most of the children, are quite naked.[7]

At the time there was peace between the Sioux and the settlers,[8] but warfare existed between the Sioux and the Pawnee tribe, traditional enemies. Dennis noticed Sioux warriors returning with the scalps of Pawnees. Mary Stuart Bailey mentioned an encounter with a Sioux Indian who wanted to know if they were armed. "He said 30 of his men were coming to kill the Pawnees. He was dressed in good style & his horse had a nice blanket also."[9] The emigrants encountered Pawnees early in the trip when the tribe was already weakened by disease and aggressive Indian enemies. They were subject to attacks by the Sioux when hunting for bison. The Pawnees traded meat with the emigrants, including bison, deer and antelope, which eventually exhausted their food supply.[10]

After Dennis and Lizzy traversed through the Plains and the Rocky Mountains, they descended into the Salt Lake valley. Dennis, always a farmer's son, was captivated by agricultural bounty there, thanks to the Mormon's use of irrigation in this place of scarce rain. Lorena Hays' account a year later expanded upon his description of the land and crops:

> Yesterday morning [we] left camp, ascended the hill, descended through a long canon [canyon] called Emigrant canon, and shortly after hove to sight of Salt Lake City. It is situated in a large valley surrounded by

7 Watson, *Hays*, 172.

8 *Ho for California*, Myres, 46, "In 1852, when [Mary] Bailey went west, the Plains tribes, particularly the Sioux, were generally peaceful," especially following the Fort Laramie Treaty of 1851. "The Mormons, although regarded with suspicion were generally hospitable to emigrants." These peaceful conditions changed after 1854 with increasing conflicts with Sioux, Cheyenne, and Arapaho Indians and direct conflict with the Mormons in the 1857-58 Utah War.

9 Bailey, 57. July 2, 1852.

10 Tate, 38-40, 45.

mountains. The valley looks tolerably green and luxuriant, but the hills or mountains have a dry, sterile appearance. The city is large, but no where [i.e. not] closely crowded, and laid off very regularly. It is well watered by streams from the mountains which are turned so as to have a pretty little brook running each side of the street, and crossing each other as do the streets….The gardens are filled with vegetables, and have a luxuriant appearance, being watered by the streams, there being little rain ever.[11]

Lorena did not stay over in Salt Lake City and Mary Stuart Bailey and her group were not allowed to enter because fear of the spread of smallpox coming in from the emigrants. However, the following day members from her company did go "to town to get some vegetables and see the City. It is said here that Governor Brigham Young was out with 73 wives last Saturday at a celebration. I will not vouch for the truth of the thing."[12]

Dennis and Lizzy lingered with the Mormons for a week in Salt Lake City. The Mormons were very hospitable to emigrants during this period, providing respite and supplies to weary travelers.[13] Similar to other travelers who passed through, Dennis and Lizzy were curious and fascinated by the Mormon practice of polygamy. They heard Brigham Young speak and met some of his wives. Although unable to find out how many wives there were, Dennis described a few encounters with Mormons, including a man who had left the religion.

Leaving Salt Lake City for travel along the Humboldt River, Mary Stuart Bailey echoed Dennis' sentiments about the difficulty of the road, writing on September 8, 1852, "We have often heard of the sand, but now we see it. No grass for the poor animals. Deep cuts through the banks through which the road goes." The next day, she observed, "The dust is awful." By the time her party reached the Humboldt Sink on September 13, "the relief station had sold out everything…"[14]

At the Humboldt Sink, before crossing the Forty Mile Desert, the road forked, the north branch on the right leading to the Truckee River and

11 Watson, *Hays* 184. July 19, 1853.

12 Bailey, 75. July 29, 1852.

13 Carvalho, Soloman Nunes, *Incidents of Travel and Adventure in the Far West with Colonel Frémont's Last Expedition* (Lincoln, University of Nebraska Press, 2004), 140-178. Photographer Carvalho, very ill from the 1853-4 Frémont expedition, spent two months recuperating in Salt Lake City, warmly hosted by Brigham Young, His journal includes many close observations of Mormon life, including multiple marriages and religious beliefs.

14 Bailey, 83-84. September 8, 9, 13, 1852.

Donner Pass. The left branch to the south directed emigrants to the Carson River Route, the path selected by the Townsends as well as the other two diarists. This trail had been forged in 1848 by the Mormon Battalion of soldiers returning to Salt Lake City from their stint in California during the Mexican–American War. The Carson River Route was shorter and less grueling than the Truckee River Route, which had twenty-seven river crossings. It became the preferred route to access California's goldfields.[15]

The Carson River valley offered refreshment to the travelers but negotiating the formidable Sierra Nevada presented the final challenge, the trail strewn with boulders, steep peaks, precipitous descents, and an increasing elevation that reached the summit at 8,600 feet. Dennis wrote that it exceeded anything that I ever imagined in "my most horrible dreams." After marveling at the beauty of the mountains, with its forests and streams, Lorena Hays described the unpredictable weather of the higher altitude:

> Cloudy and misty in the morning; rained soon and before we were at the summit, it snowed, rained and blowed. We walked much faster than the teams could ascend. Got very wet and cold while waiting for them. Two wagons were broken, one left. The ascent was long, and difficult. Near the summit we were enveloped in a cloud, so that we could see neither above or below us. A large snow bank lay along our road for some distance.[16]

In 1852, a new-cut off trail constructed along the Carson River Route provided travelers with the choice of continuing towards Placerville [known then as Hangtown] or taking a left fork off old Iron Road to Volcano, a closer destination to mining activity in the Sierra Nevada foothills. The Townsends crossed the mountain range safely, selecting the Volcano Cut-off, one of the popular places of entry to California. They arrived there on September 15, 1852 after traveling for 168 days or 5 ½ months. Soon afterwards on October 6, Mary Stuart Bailey and her party also landed in the settlement of Volcano, the same date that Dennis wrote to his family about their safe arrival.

---

15 Tortorich, Frank, "Tragedy Spring and the Opening of the Gold Rush Trail." *Amador Ledger Dispatch*, May 14, 2021, B7, Part IV, last in series of articles. See also map and text "California Trail," National Park Service, U.S. Dept. of the Interior

16 Watson, *Hays* 194-5. September 15, 1853.

Arrival in Volcano

Dennis' January 23, 1853 account of the overland journey is framed at the beginning and at the end with comments about life in Volcano. The town, located in a grassy valley, surrounded by steep mountains and piles of volcanic rock, was already a booming mining town when the Volcano Cut-Off was constructed in 1852. The Volcano Cut-off brought a stream of emigrants to Volcano, increasing the town in population and importance.[17]

As an up and coming town, Volcano now had its own newspaper, the *Volcano Weekly Ledger*. The second issue described and promoted the town:

> Among the many flourishing towns and villages which within the last six years, have sprung up as if by magic in the mining regions of California, there are few, if any, more worthy of notice than that of the town of Volcano. Its locality is on the banks of Sutter Creek, and on the northwestern margin of an irregular flat or basin, nearly of an elliptical form, and in extent varying from about half a mile to a mile in diameter. This basin is formed by a chain of high and precipitous mountains, by which it is completely surrounded, and which are all overgrown with forest trees—pine, oak and cedar—of immense size, the whole forming one of the most romantic landscape scenes to be met with anywhere....

> The town—proper, is composed of three principal streets—Main street, which runs nearly north and south, Consolation Street and Jackson. Main street is long and of respectable width, and can be made a handsome street and boasts some [structures] as extensive trading houses, and as handsome and substantial fire-proof buildings as any inland town in California.

> The commercial advantages of Volcano are very great, standing as it does in the centre of one of the richest and most extensive mining regions in the State, and with excellent roads direct to Stockton and Sacramento, as well as to the various mining camps in the vicinity.[18]

When she passed through, Mary Stuart Bailey, however, was not impressed with Volcano.

---

17 Cenotto, Larry, *Logan's Alley: Amador County Yesterdays in Picture and Prose*, Vol. IV. (Jackson, Cenotto Publications, 2003), 258-261 give a good analysis of the reasons for the Volcano cut-off and its effects on the growth of the town.

18 "A Statistical Sketch of Volcano," *Volcano Weekly Ledger*, November 3, 1852, 2.

We arrived in the first mining town in California. Took dinner there. Had a variety of vegetables. The buildings are very rude, some of logs, others framed & covered with cloth. The village is without form & prices continue very high. Saw a good many mining. It seemed like very hard work & rather low pay but some do very well.[19]

Dennis captured an image of the town, using his skills as daguerreotype photographer. Although faint and flawed, the photograph confirms the town's forested and mountainous setting, its main street featuring bulky wooden (not fire-proof brick as claimed) buildings of a commercial nature, plus a row of matching houses or stores in the foreground. Other wooden structures are scattered on the side street and in the periphery. This is likely the earliest extant photograph of Volcano, taken in fall, 1852.

The newspaper enumerated about 242 dwelling houses, including some in the process of construction. This number may have included a house that Dennis purchased soon after arrival. The Townsends lived in Volcano for several months. The area was embroiled in a frenzy of mining. In fact, the clapboard cabin where Dennis and Lizzy resided was in danger of literally being undermined. Their house was situated in a gulch where significant amounts of gold had been unearthed. It could have been near Indian Gulch or Soldier's Gulch, where many riches had been extracted.

Miner John Doble resided in Volcano at the same time and wrote a detailed journal that vividly describes the town and his life as a miner.[20] He recorded several entries regarding the arrival of emigrants, who first arrived in July in small companies on pack mules, others later coming with ox teams pulling wagons. On September 17, 1852, he observed, "Emigration still coming in rapidly. A number of women have stopped here which makes the town look quite civilized."[21] Could he have seen Lizzy?

19 Bailey, 89. October 6, 1852

20 Doble, John, *John Doble's Journal and Letters from the Mines: Mokelumne Hill, Jackson, Volcano and San Francisco, 1851-1865*, (Charles L. Camp, ed. Denver, Old West Publishing Company, 1962), 207-208. Doble's journal covered life in Volcano from 1852-February 11, 1854 (although he lived there until 1861). He was twice elected Justice of the Peace for Township 3 (Volcano area) from September 1857-1859. In October 1861 he was elected Associate Judge of the Court of Sessions at Jackson, Amador County. See editor's note #22, 300 for Volcano's origin of name and geology.

21 Doble, 115.

Doble described placer mining, involving separating gold from river gravels. In a rich lead at Indian Gulch that extended for 200 yards, miners were "sinking holes & tunneling from the Gulch & taking out the dirt and piling [it] along the Gulch to wash when the rain comes again as the water has all run off here."[22] Throughout his journal he wrote about the day-to day-hard work of prospecting, digging holes and tunnels, and dealing with water, dirt and mud to extract the flecks of gold among the gravel. For example, on Jan. 16th 1853,

> The last few days we have been sluiceing [sluicing] with a ground sluice that is to dig the dirt down in the Gulch & wash it [in] the ground then shovel up and out of that on to the sand & gravel & wash it in the tom... in this way the gold generally settles on the bottom...[23]

Dennis was not immune to mining for gold and tried his hand at this exhausting, dirty work. But his letter of January 23, 1852, he made it clear that the mining life was not for him—he felt much more attuned to farming and growing crops. After all, he was an educated man and the son of a farmer. Lizzy however, was fascinated enough by mining and its equipment to make a model of a rocker or Tom[24] for Dennis to send to his family. In this letter, Dennis (or perhaps Lizzy) described in detail the workings of this essential tool for placer mining.

With his interest in farming, Dennis saw California's potential in agriculture when most were focused on mining as a source of riches. The letter is particularly significant in that it states the Townsends' reason for coming to California—health not wealth. For a chronically ill person like Dennis, hearing reports of its mild climate from other emigrants was certainly a major incentive to make the overland journey.

Unfortunately that winter of 1852 was especially harsh in Volcano. Dennis wrote of impassable roads, rising prices, and dwindling supplies. The journal of John Doble confirms the severity of the winter with high prices and shortages in Volcano. Starting December 15, Doble wrote

---

22   Doble, 105. June 27, 1852

23   Doble, 139

24   http://www.actforlibraries.org/using-the-long-tom-in-gold-mining/. The long Tom supplanted the cradle or rocker which was used by a single person. Lizzy replicated a rocker box, smaller than the long Tom which was operated by four men, having a washing box 6 to 12 feet long.

about heavy snow and rain that eventually washed away bridges. On Sunday, December 26, he related,[25]

> Last Sunday a man in Liquor attempted to cross the creek & fell in & was carried down by the current & was drowned & his body is yet not found...The banks along Soldier's Gulch are falling to a great extent... the Graveyard which was about 200 feet square has most all fallen in also...in front of Town about 200 feet of the hill has slid in also...several other places of from 100 to 150 have slid in...Provision is getting very scarce in town...

Although the snow melted by the end of the year, heavy rains continued through mid-January, creating additional misery. It took two more months for the Townsends to decide to move on.

As mentioned earlier, at the end of his long letter of January 23, 1853, Dennis' script emerges in the last page with his signature, comments and inquiries about various members of the family. He responded to mail from some of them, already retrieved by him from Sacramento. He asked about his brother Alfred in Texas, mentioned Alstyne, Isabelle, Torrey, Elmer, Orson, answered questions from sisters Susan and Eliza, and hoped to receive a note from Velette and Marquis, the youngest of the siblings. No mention was made of William, whom he may have written to earlier. He requested that this letter be passed on to other siblings living in New England. This letter expresses his concern and affection for individuals in this large family who remained close across the expanding nation.

---

25 Doble, 135.

Letters: 1852 – 1853

Camp 2 miles from St. Joseph May 1ˢᵗ 1852

Dear Br. Wm.[William]

Here we have been lying a week for grass to grow. Next Monday we intend to risk it and cross the Missouri. There has been a great rush at the ferry for the last 10 days though some advise waiting until the 10th of this month, and say the foremost teams will suffer for want of feed. We have met with no serious accident yet. Lizzy and I have not suffered by the trip in respect to health. Mc's wife has been sick from the day that she started. She has a very bad cold and cough. Her child is also afflicted in the same way. These circumstances make more work for Lizzy than I like, but she gets along very well. Most of our route lay though what Suckers[1] would consider a barren country but from about 100 miles back to this place there is an excellent farming country, rich rolling prairie mostly. The whole expense of our team for lots, feed and ferriage, up to date has amounted to $45. [At] New Brunswick on the Missouri, we paid 75 cents per bushel for corn. We have found feed cheaper here than at any other place in the state.[2] Corn 25 cents per bush, and hay 50 cents per hundred. The prices of provisions here are but little in advance of St. Louis prices say, just about the freight. St. Joseph contains about 4,000 inhabitants and has the appearance of a rapidly growing place.[3] The California and Oregon emigration, the fruitful country around it, besides the Hannibal and St. Joseph railroad,[4] which I learn has been taken by a company and is to be completed if I mistake not in 3 years, must at a future day render it an important city. Californians are starting out in various fashions. Several have gone with wheel-barrows and hand-

---

1 Sucker State was a 19th century name for Illinois. There are several explanations for the name, such as those who rushed for employment when the first lead mine opened in Galena, Illinois. https://illinoistimes.com/article-895-the-sucker-state.

2 Unruh, *The Plains Across*, 112-113. Prices of provisions fluctuated during the March-May outfitting season. In Independence Missouri, the price for a yoke (pair) of oxen varied from $40 in mid-March to $50-$65 at the beginning of April, with a range of $45-$60 by late May.

3 Unruh,115. St. Joseph grew from a population of 682 in 1845 to 1,500 in 1848, to more than 3,000 in the early 1850s. As Townsend remarked, the population continued to rise: 8,932 inhabitants by 1860.

4 The Hannibal and St. Joseph Railroad was the first to cross Missouri starting in Hannibal and going to St. Joseph, Missouri, reducing the time to get to St. Joseph.

barrows. The hand-barrow is calculated for 3 or 4 persons.[5] Some pull and some push. They carry provisions enough and a small tent. A day or two ago it was reported that some emigrant[6] had killed an Indian and that the Indians killed 3 of the whites not far from St. Jos. but I think it false. While Buck Blackshare's[7] company were herding their cattle on the Missouri bottom the Indians killed one of their oxen. They want the emigrants to move on as soon as they cross the river and not ly [lie] by to herd their cattle. Anderson Hedrick came just in time to relieve the boys as they were short of money and had to purchase another ox to take the place of the one that was killed. The company has moved on and probably nearly all the other Greene County boys. Lizzy and I walked to town today, did some shopping, went down to the ferry and nocked [knocked] about among the emigrants and Indians a while and returned very tired—that is Lizzy was tired I mean. While we were going in Ed Simmons and Charly Rogers overtook us. We had not seen them before. They are going by Council Bluffs [Iowa].[8] Ben got in 2 days before us. He is fat, saucy and in good spirits. The prospect is that the emigration will not be near as large this year from this point as in 1850. Some men are going out with a "pocket full of rocks" with the intention of purchasing cattle of the emigrants 200 or 300 miles this side of the gold region to drive in and speculate upon. Tell the children that I remember them affectionately. Mag's and Martha's[9] Easter eggs arrived in safety. I hope that they together with Wilford John Eliza Mary Jane, and Monroe will improve their minds as fast as possible. I suppose that Mr. Russell is flourishing gloriously. How I love the old gentleman.[10] I must write him an affectionate

5   Unruh,107. A "wheelbarrow train" consisting of 5 Irishmen carrying their supplies in a handcart departed for California from Independence about May 1, 1852. Wheelbarrows were used by Mormon settlers in later years. *Volcano Weekly Ledger*, June 9, 1856, 1, "500 Mormon handcart pioneers leave Iowa City for Salt Lake City, Utah, carrying all their possessions in two-wheeled handcarts."

6   Townsend struck out these words --"the whites" had killed an Indian.

7   Greene County Historical & Genealogical Society found no reference to Buck Blackshare or his company in the Census or Carrollton Gazette newspaper prior to May 1852. His first name may have been William.

8   Unruh, 98. Council Bluffs was the northernmost jumping-off point, 40 miles west of St. Joseph and closer to the intersection of the Missouri and Platte Rivers.

9   This refers to brother William's second wife, Martha and her daughter Margaret by her first husband. Dennis expresses his conviction that children (other names unknown) and family members pursue education.

10   John Russell, age 56, is listed in the 1850 Census as a teacher living with Dennis and Lizzy in Carrollton, Illinois. Russell was also from Vermont. He would have seemed old to Dennis who was in his early 30s.

letter ere long for I cannot possibly stand it long without holding some kind of communication with the modest sweet meek and lovely man. I hope you are arranging your affairs to emigrate next spring. Lots of families are going this year. The country for miles back from St. Joe is dotted all over with wagons and tents. I shall not write you again before leaving the States. My whiskers are getting long and a thunder-storm is coming up. Our tent shed rain and the hogs sometimes hook an ear of our corn. Ben sends his love to all the children May included and my corns are all improving. The boys are popping their revolvers all around me and I didn't like that tough squirrel for dinner.

Your aff'te Br.

Dennis Townsend

UTAustin/VHS MSC133:8

Volcano, Calaveras County, Ca. Oct. 6, 1852

Dear Parents, Brothers & Sisters,

We arrived here safe on the 15th of September in better health than when we started but <u>tired</u>, <u>tired</u>, **tired**. Started with 5 yoke of oxen and got in with three. Were 168 days on the road. The particulars of our journey I must omit until next time. Volcano is a mining town. Miners are digging close to our house and we know not but the house stands over a pile [of gold]. Times are dull just now on account of scarcity of water for gold washing. Wages which have been until recently $5 per day are now only $3. Living is very high here which is a great drawback unless a person is making money rapidly. When I get a little more settled and the bile on my ankle gets well I will enter more into particulars. I was very happy to get a letter from you directed to Sacramento and also one from Wm. Please direct the next to Volcano, Calaveras County.[11] I suppose that California seems a long distance from you. If [distance] is reckoned [not] in miles but in time, it is not far off. Notice the date of this letter and the time when you receive it, and you will perceive that the distance is quickly annihilated. Write often. Wishing you health and happiness I remain,
Yours affectionately,

Dennis Townsend

---

11 Letters to Dennis from his family were delivered and retrieved in Sacramento. Since Volcano had a Post Office, mail could be delivered directly there. Volcano was originally in Calaveras County, but in July, 1854 it became part of the new Amador County.

Volcano, Jan. 23, 1853

Dear Parents, Brothers & Sisters[12]

I hasten to answer your letters rec'd last mail. I was much rejoiced to learn that you are all well and flourishing. Time flies and the past seems like a dream. Is it possible father that you are 72 years of age; that nearly forty years have passed over your head, Susan [sister], and sprinkled it with grey, that your brother Dennis is now bowing a bald head over this shirt, that my younger brothers and sisters are all full grown men and women even to Marquis, the baby, and most of them married each with a home of his own? Yet it is even so. The world will not stand still and it stands us in hand as we advance to keep in the right course so that we may be happy in every period of life and peacefully resign the world at its close Father, I thank you for your advice and will attend to it. Our design in coming to Ca. was not entirely to get rich: The healthiness of the climate was one grand inducement though I am aware that a person may have bad health in any climate by wrong living. Since our arrival here up to about Dec. the weather was most delightful and after that we had long and severe rain storms besides a storm of snow which was not melted for two or three days, a thing never known here before. The roads became almost impassable and the prices of provisions were so high, in consequence of the difficulty in transportation that a miner had to do pretty well to buy enough to eat. In some places farther back in the mountains we heard of people being on the point of starvation. The pinch is over now I think. There was plenty in Volcano but prices were somewhat up, 80 cents per pound for flour, 75 cents for pickled pork, 50 cents for cornmeal, one dollar for butter, etc.

(2)   Not withstanding all drawbacks I have been able to save something above expenses. Houses in the mines are of a very frail nature either made of logs or posts driven into the ground enclosed and covered by rough clapboards just as they are split from the pine. The country is heavily wooded principally with pine and oak. We are living here comfortably in a clapboard cabin which I bought immediately after we got in. It is a little out of town in a gulch from which many thousands of the shining dust have been taken. The ground has been dug up within a few feet of our door and we don't

---

12 My transcription of this long letter includes the page numbers indicated in the original letter. Curiously, the handwriting in all the pages (except pg. 8) is very different than Dennis' usual script, which varied from elegant and angular to scrawling, always leaning to the right. Here the letters and words are rounded and leaning left. The style and content still display Dennis' careful choice of words with many words crossed out and re-phrased, but the penmanship may have been Lizzy's.

know but our house will be under mined yet. Miners claims are paramount to all others. If a "lead" runs into your yard or under your house they have the privilege of working it out. There is but little ground in the mines fit for cultivation on account of the dryness of the summers but where the ground can be irrigated it produces very abundantly. I never saw so excellent vegetables as grow here, and gardening, where a patch of ground can be obtained in the mines, is very profitable. $2000 worth of potatoes, for example, and even more are often produced on a single acre.[13] It requires 2 or 3 thousand dollars to commence farming operations on a modest scale. I intend to quit mining as soon as I can decently. The mines are filled with people from all quarters. I see people from New England every day and I am working with a man originally from Vermont. It would take me a week to give you the particulars of our journey across the plains. Between St. Joseph and Fort Kearney nine miles below which we strike the Platt [River], our route lay through a beautiful undulating prairie country occasionally crossing a stream running through a charming valley. The lands seemed to be rich.

(3)Here we encountered rain, wolves, Lac [Lakota] Iowa[14] and Pawnee Indians but escaped unhurt though I could tell you tales of sickness, murder, and hair breadth escapes that came to our knowledge as we were passing from Fort Kearney to Fort Laramie; up the Platt [River] bottom we had the finest road that I ever saw for the distance, hard and level. Here is the country of the Sioux. These are the finest looking Indians we saw on the road. A company of warriors passed us with scalps and booty they had just taken in a fight with the Pawnees. This part of our journey would have been very pleasant had it not been for sickness.[15] West of Fort Laramie we heard of but little sickness, our route here lay over the Black Hills which are dreaded simply on account of the roughness of the road which in places is

13 [Mason, Jesse D.] *History of Amador County, California, with Illustrations and Biographical Sketches of its Prominent Men and Pioneers.* (Oakland, Thompson and West, 1881), 206. In 1851, James L. Halstead and Thomas Bryant raised potatoes on the lower part of a ranch next to the town of Volcano. In 1852, Henry Jones planted several acres of potatoes on the upper ranch.

14 The Lakota are the westernmost Sioux. They became the most powerful tribe on the Plains by the 1850s.

15 Tate, *Encounters*, 132. Cholera flourished between the crowded jumping-off camps along the Missouri River, where it was often contracted, and Fort Laramie. Most of the deaths from the disease occurred along the Nebraska section of the Platte River Trail. *Ho for California*, Myres. 42, "The most frequent cause of death on the trail was disease. Cholera, smallpox, intestinal disorders, and scurvy were common."

steep and rocky but no worse than I have seen in New England. In fact we had much worse road beyond the Rocky Mountains as we approached Salt Lake. The pass [South Pass] through the Rocky Mountains is a gradually inclined plain with a very good road. Here we camped on the night of the 4th of July. A little snow fell in the night. At a short distance were in view [of] mountains covered with snow. Just before reaching Salt Lake valley we pass over two very high and difficult mountains. The valley is very beautiful enclosed with very steep, lofty mountains with very sharp peaks capped with snow the year round. The Mormons could not have chosen a more secluded spot. Their lands are very productive but require irrigation as it never rains any of consequence in the valley. During our week's stay there were several heavy thunderstorms on every side upon the mountains but only a slight

(4) sprinkle in the valley. Streams of pure cold water run from the mountains though all parts of the valley which renders it very easy for farmers to irrigate their lands. Such fields of wheat I never saw in any country, perfectly even, none too thick, none too thin, and none lodged. They can raise better crops for not having rain, for they can regulate the watering of their lands just as they wish. Ninety bushels of wheat have been raised from an acre there. They cannot raise good corn. I attended church and their great celebration on the 24th of July, the anniversary of their arrival in Salt Lake valley. Heard Brigham Young speak, the man who had wives and children scattered over all their settlements. I saw several of his wives and my wife visited at a place where there were two or three and while she was there. Young came with another one or two when there was a great shaking of hands among his wives. Every Mormon has all the wives that he pleases provided he can support them. One man had a mother and daughter and each of them had a young babe. I asked a Mormon how many wives Brigham Young had and was answered, "A considerable many but he did not know how many."[16] He has a fine house in the city and another appropriated to his wives each having a room by herself. A man who was once a Mormon and had left them informed me that at the time of the Mexican War, Young seduced the wife of one of his brethren who was absent on military duty. He made her believe that she would be damned unless she became his spiritual wife. If a woman demands salvation of a man, by their doctrine, he is bound to take her as his spiritual side [*following words written in margins*] and become responsible for her salvation.

16 Carvalho, 175. The photographer Solomon Nunes Carvalho, staying with the Mormons in spring, 1864, heard from a niece that Brigham Young had 19 wives and thirty-three children, some whom were adults. Carvalho met 11 of Young's wives at different times, "all of them are beautiful women."

(5) From Salt Lake through to Ca. it is considered much the hardest part of the trip on account of scarcity of feed, bad water and bad road. However, there seems to be less sickness on this part of the road, and this year, the latter part of the emigration found plenty of feed most of the way until we arrived within 60 miles of the Sink of the Humboldt, but from some cause teams began to go down when they struck the head waters of this river. At the Sink the 40 <u>mile</u> desert commences where the road is lined from beginning to end with carcases [carcasses] of oxen, cows, mules and horses, nearly all of which died there in /49 and/50. They are not in the least decayed but completely dried. This year there were several trading posts where failing cattle were bought or picked up and furnished with feed & water. We sold a yoke of cattle there for ten dollars. On leaving the desert you arrive at Carson river bordered with heavy timber and furnishing clear cool excellent water. None but the traveller can appreciate the effect of the transition. For weeks your road has been like a bed of ashes whose dust has inflicted perpetual suffocation, your prospect naked mountains without a single shrub except here and there a cedar bush and a lonesome valley through which winds a sluggish poisonous stream lined with willows. Not a drop of good water have you tasted and to conclude all a desert of 40 miles presenting a continuous picture of desolation and death; but now you gaze upon a beautiful and fruitful valley, listen to the birds singing among the branches of gigantic forest trees and drink the cool sparkling water. We travel up the Carson river and follow up a branch on the right through a narrow rocky Canion [canyon] between mountains of astonishing height, where it is said the emigrant sees the entire "<u>elephant</u>"[17] in the distance of 6 miles. The passage exceeds anything that I ever imagined in my most horrible dreams.

(6) You would not suppose it possible for a team to get through. After this we have to climb the Sierra Nevada into the region of eternal winter over a road of similar description to the canion, rough, rocky, steep and more difficult than a Yankee could guess. Having crossed these mountains without accident we are safely in Ca, the land of shining dust. Serene skies, fruitful valleys, charming landscapes and romantic mountain scenery. In crossing the plains I dreaded the rivers the <u>worst</u> but we crossed them all in safety though many were drowned both at the Platt and Green river fords and ferries. We forded the South fork of the Platt, crossed Laramie fork on

17 Levy, Jo Ann, *They Saw the Elephant: Women in the California Gold Rush* (Norman, University of Oklahoma Press, 1992), xvi. "For gold rushers, the elephant symbolized both the high cost of their endeavor—the myriad possibilities for misfortune on the journey or in California—and, like the farmer's circus elephant, an exotic sight, an unequaled experience, the adventure of a lifetime."

a new bridge, the North fork of the main Platt on a kind of boat formed of 5 log canoes pinned together, forded the Sweetwater many times, ferried over Green river in an excellent boat owned by the Mormons and ferried and forded other rivers too numerous to mention. I could speak of many curiosities we saw on the way but will not at present. I hope you will be satisfied with this faint outline and imperfect sketch of our journey. This letter is to all of you including Orson and Alstyne. Mother you have no idea how much pleasure your letter afforded me, on account of the picture of matters and things connected with my old home and the particulars about my acquaintances. I rejoice to hear that your health has improved under your new treatment. I had access to the *Water Cure Journal* the year before we came here and practiced the system to a considerable extent in relation to diet and bathing.[18] Both myself and wife are much opposed to the popular system of drugging [taking medication]. My wife had the prevailing disease on the Platt which swept off so many.[19] She could not be prevailed on to take medicine but she staved out the disease.

(7) My wife's name was Elizabeth Ray before she was married. I call her Lizzy for shortness, but you may call her what you please. Lizzy has made the model of a Tom & Riffle box to send you, an instrument used in gold washing. The Tom consists of a trough of wood with what is termed a shirt iron screen or riddle at the end. The Tom is to be set with the riddle directly over the Riffle bar and so inclined that the water will pass first through it. The dirt is stirred in the Tom by a shovel or hoe until it is washed completely from the stones and gold. The gold, small stones, and gravel pass through the riddle into the Riffle box. The dirt runs off with the water and the large stones remain on the riddle and are thrown out by the shovel. The gold being the heaviest sinks to the bottom of the box and there remains; the force of water instantly washes over the gravel so that it is all the time just on a level with the lower edge of the box, which is also set a little inclined. When you have finished washing, you pan out the gold in your riffle box and all is done. Lizzy also sends you a specimen of the dust and two locks of hair which you will please accept with much love from us both. I should have said the holes in the riddle are about ½ inch in diameter and arranged not in

18 Watson, *Hays*, editor's notes, 399. Hydropathy or the water-cure was a "popular and widespread medical reform movement [that] treated the whole person, internally as well as externally, rather than just symptoms. *The Water-Cure Journal*, founded in 1845 with the motto, 'Wash and be Healed,' also supported women's rights and temperance." Townsend and his wife preferred this more holistic method to taking medications (drugging).

19 This may have been cholera.

the form represented in the model, for in that case it would be possible for the gold to pass down the riddle without meeting a hole. The holes should be in this form [*square diagram with row of 4 dots alternating with 3 in next row.*]

I had not heard that Alfred had returned from Texas. Please give me particulars. I wrote to him twice but rec'd no answer. I wish he would come to this country and go into business with me. The climate would exactly suit him. The next time you write have Valette and Marquis put in something. Susan, we did not have to eat our cattle to keep from starving on the Plains. Eliza, the society is passable here but not the most refined. The Methodists have a church here and hold frequent meetings.

(8) [20]I am glad to hear of the prosperity of Alstyne, Isabel, & Torrey. My wife will write next time. We shall expect another letter from you as soon as practicable. Tell us how Elmer, Orson and all the rest are doing. Live right and "throw drugs to the dogs."

Yours Affectionately

Dennis Townsend [flourishes below the D]

p.s. Eliza. You have my thanks for the interest you manifest in the preservation of my health. I believe the *Water Cure Journal* is calculated to do much good but I have neglected to subscribe for any periodicals yet as I have not felt myself settled here for any length of time.

DT

Brother Alstyne. After reading this will you give Orson an opportunity to do the same & then send it to Susan. Hoping you will attend to it as soon as possible as Susan in anxious to get it.—Her address is Clinton, Mass.—if you please you may direct to the care of G.P. Smith as she may get it sooner We are all as well as usual.[21]

---

20 The handwriting here is different than in the body of the letter, varying in each of the three paragraphs. The first paragraph slants to the right, and the signature is consistent with others signed by Dennis.

21 This insert by Dennis appears to be hastily added, scrawled in pencil. The last sentence is written vertically in the left margin.

Figure 4. Indian Encampment near Fort Laramie Wyoming: *National Museum of the American Indian, Smithsonian Institution, P010119*

Figure 5. Lakota men, women and children at Fort Laramie for 1868 Treaty: *National Museum of the American Indian, Smithsonian Institution, P15378*

Figure 6. Volcano, 1852 by Dennis Townsend: *Dolph Briscoe Center for American History, The University of Texas at Austin*

Figure 7. A Miner using the Rocker: *Courtesy of the California History Room, California State Library, Sacramento, California*

7 My wife's name was Elizabeth Ray before she was married I call
her Lizzy for shortness. but you may call her what you please
Lizzy has made the model of a Tom & Riffle box to send you
an instrument used in Gold washing. The Tom consists of a trough
of wood with what is termed a sheet iron screen or riddle at the
end. The Tom is to be set with the riddle ~~~~~~~ directly over
the Riffle box and so inclined that the water will pass freely
through it. The dirt is stirred in the Tom by a shovel or hoe until it
is washed completly from the stones ~~~~ gold. The gold
small stones and gravel pass through the riddle into the Riffle
box. the dirt runs off with the water and the large stones remain
on the riddle and are thrown out by the shovel. The gold being
the heaviest sinks to the bottom of the box and there remains
the force of the water constantly washes over the gravel so that
it is all the time just on a level with the lower edge of the
box which is also set a little inclined. When you have
finished washing you pan out the gold in your riffle box
and all is done. Lizzy also sends you a specimen of the
dust and two locks of hair ~~~~~ which you will please
accept with much love from us both. I should have said
the holes in the riddle are about 1/2 inch in diameter and
arranged not in the form represented in the model for in
that case it would be possible for the gold to pass down
the riddle without meeting a hole. The holes should be
in this form :::::: I had not heard that Alfred had returned from Texas. Please give me particulars I wrote to
him twice in Texas but rec'd no answer. I wish he would
come to this country and go into business with me. The climate
would exactly suit him. The next time you write have
Villette and Marquis put in something. Susan, we did
not have bread nor Cattle to keep from starving on the plains
Eliza the society is passable here, but not the most refined
The Methodists have a church here and hold frequent meetings

Figure 8. Letter to Family, January 23, 1853: *Dennis Townsend Papers, 1833-1858 (camh-dob-009558_0007_pub), Dolph Briscoe Center for American History, The University of Texas at Austin*

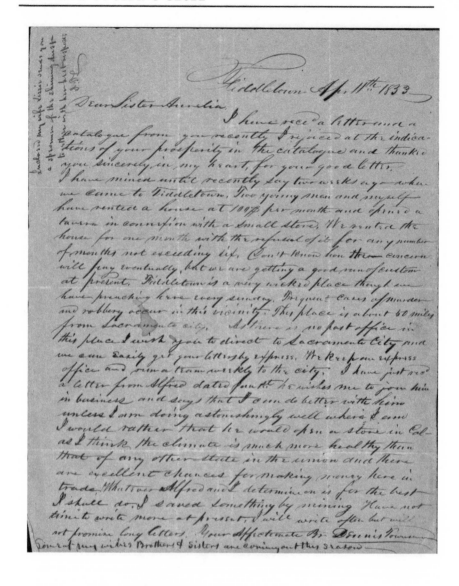

Figure 9. Letter to Aurelia, April 11, 1853: *Dennis Townsend Papers, 1833-1858 (camh-dob-009559_0001_pub), Dolph Briscoe Center for American History, The University of Texas at Austin*

CHAPTER 3

Settling in Fiddletown

Arrival in Fiddletown 1853-4

The brutal winter in Volcano may have been the main incentive for the Townsends to move to Fiddletown at the end of March, 1853. With an elevation of 1683 feet, Fiddletown is set at a lower level in the Sierra Nevada foothills than Volcano at 2070 feet, its climate lacking heavy snow. Dennis and Lizzy would have taken the stage road from Volcano leading to Fiddletown. Although Dennis did not allude to the conveyance they took, assuredly the ride was bumpy, first heading north out of Volcano's hollow and then west down, down, the hills along a rough trail filled with rocks, depressions and sharp curves. Fiddletown is located in a narrow pass following the north fork of Dry Creek on one side and rolling hills studded with oaks and pines on opposite south side. The town served as a commercial hub for nearby mining camps and was situated closer than Volcano to the city of Sacramento, 45-50 miles to the southwest and accessible through Fiddletown-Sacramento Road.[1]

The Townsends resided in Fiddletown for the rest of the decade. Dennis' letters are notable in providing a first-person account of a raucous Gold Rush mining town that transitioned into a settled community, its population increasing with families arriving overland and by steamships landed in San Francisco. The new emigrants joined the miners, merchants and adventurers who had already discovered rich placer diggings in the surroundings. Miners extracted gold from Dry Creek, from ancient dry river beds in the vicinity, and in the gulches and ravines of the hills surrounding the town. Dry Creek, paralleling the Main Street, lived up to its name—for most of the year, especially in the heat of summer it became parched like the land around it. Water in the creek became abundant only during the winter and even that was unpredictable.

---

1 Zorbas, Elaine, *Fiddletown: From Gold Rush to Rediscovery* (Altadena, Mythos Press, 1997). See chapter, "Travel to Fiddletown and Beyond," 36-41. The distance then between Volcano and Fiddletown was at least 20 miles (now 17 miles by car). According to Carson River Trail expert Frank Tortorich, the junction leading to each town (now Shake Ridge Road and Fiddletown Road) was likely to east of the current location. From Sacramento, the road headed southeast to the foothills, passing through the town of Plymouth, then called Puckerville, about 8 miles west of Fiddletown.

The four letters written by Dennis in 1853 show a town with substantial commercial development and a diverse population estimated at 1500. Shortly after arriving in Fiddletown, Dennis wrote to his sister Aurelia on April 11, 1853 that it was "a very wicked place" with frequent murders and robberies in the area. By November, the "society had improved."

Dennis' November 18, 1853 letter to his mother, Susan and Eliza provides the earliest known record of Fiddletown's commercial activity. He counted the number of stores and also enumerated the bakeries (one was owned by the Frenchman Augustus Legendre), restaurants, taverns, carpenter's and blacksmith's shops. He did not mention the Union Hotel or the U.S. Hotel both present in Fiddletown since 1852, nor did he mention the saloons, gambling establishments and brothels that arose in most early predominantly male settlements.[2] At the time, Dennis and Lizzy were working in a tavern or inn that offered food and lodging to the public.

Dennis focused on the presence of churches as a civilizing force. In 1852 both Fiddletown and Volcano established Methodist–Episcopal churches.[3] Methodist ministers travelled on a circuit to the various mining camps and towns; preaching in Fiddletown occurred every two weeks. The Temperance Movement reached both towns, addressing the dissolute behavior and drunkenness pervasive in mining areas. John Doble reported on Temperance meetings as well as meetings at the Methodist Church. He observed that the "Meetings of both kinds have been well attended & the Temperance order is increasing rapidly."[4] Fiddletown established a chapter of the Sons of Temperance in 1854. The Townsends attended church services but were not active in the temperance movement. In one letter, Dennis declares his approval for Vermont's legislative attempts to restrain intemperance, adding that "California beats all the places for drinking."[5]

Festive balls held in both towns gave the opportunity for men and women to socialize. John Doble described a ball he attended on April 11, 1853:

> I went to the Ball last night& and stayed all night…came home at daylight & then slept away the most of the forenoon….The Company consisted of 14 women & 37 men and time passed verry [very] agreeable & everything went off much the same as such things generally do. The supper was excellent consisting in part of Oyster soup. Candies, Pound

2 Zorbas, see 5-15 and other chapters for early development of Fiddletown. There is no tally of these less respectable establishments which do appear in later Fiddletown accounts.

3 Cenotto, *Logan's Alley*, Vol. II, 29-30.

4 Doble, 182, October 4, 1853.

5 Dennis Townsend to William Townsend, May 17, 1853. P.S. to Van Buren.

cake, etc. etc....I feel very stupid today.[6]

The following year Lorena Hays was whisked from the community of Willow Springs to a ball in Fiddletown:

> The party was very pleasant and enjoyed by most present. Fiddletown looks like a thriving and prosperous place, but is not a very pretty place or handsomely located, being situated in a narrow ravine with only room for one street and that is very narrow.[7]

In the same November 18 letter, Dennis described dealing with different races and nationalities: Indians, Negroes, Chinese and Mexicans. The Gold Rush had attracted people from around the world, who encountered each other for the first time, not always to the liking of Americans or each other. Representatives from many different countries and states settled in Fiddletown, including people from the British Isles, Western Europe, Mexico, Chile, Australia, and China, joining the Mexicans and Native Americans who were first there. [8] In an added note to a letter penned to his father on May 17, 1853 Dennis tells his youngest brother Marquis of the presence of "thousands of Chinese," referring to them as weak, preyed upon by Indians, even mentioning a recent murder committed. Chinese and Native Americans both faced mistreatment and violence from prejudiced whites. Yet based on this observation, Native Americans—an oppressed group whose territory was being invaded by outsiders—attacked the Chinese, another vulnerable group. By November with more exposure to the Chinese, Dennis expressed a mixture of curiosity and fascination with them and their customs of dressing, eating rice and drinking tea, portraying the Chinese in the context of a new exciting world, full of wonders.

The Chinese were a sizable component of Fiddletown's population starting 1852 when many people living in Guangdong Province, close to Hong Kong, made the arduous journey from southeastern China to California in search of gold. By the mid-1850s, Chinese residents had established their own community on the west part of Main Street and remained an important presence in Fiddletown throughout the 19th century.[9] The Main

6 Doble, 152.

7 Watson, *Hays, 203 and* 241, May 17, 1854. Full account reproduced in Zorbas, *Fiddletown*, 25. The community of Willow Springs was located along the main road from Sacramento leading to Fiddletown.

8 Zorbas, *Fiddletown*, 6, and "From China to Fiddletown, 30-35.

9 Zorbas, *Banished and Embraced: The Chinese in Fiddletown and the Mother Lode* (Plymouth, Mythos Press, 2015). The book covers the development and activities of the Chinese community in Fiddletown and Amador County. See chapter "The Fiddletown Chinese Community Develops," 35-40. By 1860, Chinese were at least 1/3 of the

Street commercial section was divided—Chinese on the west, Americans and Europeans on the east. Still, trade took place between these two sectors. Yet after his early observations, Dennis did not refer to the town's Chinese population. Although he worked in various endeavors, he may not have had direct contact with its Chinese residents in a way that impacted his life or he may have not given them notice, "an invisible presence."

As for mining, Dennis had given it a try in Volcano. He wasn't seduced by illusions of sudden wealth nor taken in by the lure of gold. Besides the difficulty of digging for and retrieving gold, scarcity of water during California's long dry seasons made profiting from mining an unstable enterprise. As mentioned in several of Dennis' letters, when mining was slow, business in Fiddletown was also slow. California's salubrious climate and the potential of improved health had motivated Dennis and Lizzy to make the cross country journey, not dreams of wealth.

Dennis viewed California through the eyes of a Vermonter coming from a harsh climate and unyielding soil. As a son of a farmer, he was attentive to agricultural potential of California, enhanced by its favorable climate. Especially when writing to his father, Dennis extolled the quality and size of vegetables and flowers. He always looked at the potential of farming, noting that the higher prices obtained for produce made growing profitable. Yet he underestimated the areas in Fiddletown appropriate for cultivation. During the 1850s, new settlers cleared many acres of trees and brush to make room for growing crops and raising livestock. Accompanying mining, agriculture flourished in the foothills, providing settlers with fresh fruit and vegetables.[10]

Although urged and sometimes tempted by his brother Albert to join him in Texas, Dennis felt that California offered better opportunities for making a living. Yet he did not encourage his family to make the long overland journey to California. Lizzy's family was more adventurous with two sisters (one married) and a brother arriving in Fiddletown about six months after Lizzy and Dennis.

Correspondence from California with faraway family

The extended Townsend family faithfully kept in touch with each other through letters after the siblings scattered to various parts of the country.

population in Fiddletown.

10 Zorbas, *Fiddletown*, Chapter "Bounty from the Earth," 60-64.

By relocating to California, Dennis moved the farthest away, 3,000 miles distance from Vermont—at the other end of the continent.

Dennis wrote letters to his family from Fiddletown from 1853-1862. His sister, Aurelia Herrick, who remained in New England, received the preponderance of his California letters. She was his oldest sister and his most constant correspondent. In 1847, she was living in Fitzwilliam, New Hampshire with her husband Horace Herrick, who headed up a school. She also taught in the school. Ten years later, they moved to Montpelier, Vermont, where Mr. Herrick, also a Reverend, went into business.[11] Aurelia relayed news of the family to the other siblings, including Dennis.

Following the Gold Rush, letters and newspapers from the East and South arrived by steamship after a voyage from New York to San Francisco that could take up to three or more months depending on whether the route was around Cape Horn (the longest trip), via the Nicaragua Isthmus, or by crossing the Isthmus of Panama, which became the preferred route. Steamships sailed from New York to Chagres, Panama. Passengers and mail then had to disembark, crossing the Isthmus by canoe along the Chagres River, followed by mule or horse transportation through the jungle. On this treacherous seventy mile journey, tropical diseases were rampant and accidents common. Once reaching Panama City, the final part of the trip involved awaiting another steamship that traversed the Pacific from Panama City to San Francisco. The Pacific Mail Steamship Company received a subsidized contract from the U.S. Postal Department for the Pacific route in 1850, with instructions to increase sailings to the 1st and 15th of the month.[12]

In 1849, thousands of letters and newspapers overwhelmed the new Post Office in San Francisco which was not equipped to handle the barrage and distribute it to the mining interior. In June, 1850 Sacramento became the second point of mail distribution, but local post offices were slow to be established. [13] Private express companies arose to fill the void and deliver mail, packages, newspapers, and gold dust to and from the mining areas to the distribution centers.

Fiddletown lacked a post office when the Townsends arrived in April 1853. According to Lizzy's recollection many years later, Dennis walked

11 Meacham, 14 and 19. Herrick's business is not specified.
12 Coburn, Jesse L., *Letters of Gold: California Postal History through 1869* (U.S. Philatelic Classic Society, Inc. 1864). See Chapter 4, 'Early California Steamship Mail,' 81- 103. The U.S. Mail Steamship Company received the contract for delivery between New York and Chagres. These companies and others competed for routes in the early 1850s, shortening the length and expense for steamship travel.
13 Coburn, 45-48.

the winding, hilly road leading to Drytown to retrieve the first Sacramento mail to Fiddletown, consisting of two letters and a newspaper.[14] Yet a local express office was conveniently located at the inn or public house (tavern) and store in which the Townsends lived and worked. In letters written in November, 1853, Dennis instructed his sister Aurelia and his father to address letters to Sacramento City, an estimated 50 miles away. A team from the express office picked up mail weekly there and delivered it to the office in Fiddletown, relieving Dennis from making the trip to the city or to Drytown, which never did get a post office [15]

Meanwhile, a petition had been sent to Washington for a new post office in Fiddletown. Recruitment of new postmasters in California was hampered by low pay and high living expenses.[16] Still, Dennis eagerly awaited the official response with expectation that he would be appointed as Postmaster. When Fiddletown Post Office was established on the last day of December, 1853, Dennis Townsend became its first Postmaster, a position he held through 1861. Fiddletown was then part of El Dorado County, located on its southern border, later conveyed to Amador County in April 16, 1855.[17]

Developments in Fiddletown and Around

Before his appointment as Postmaster, Dennis had opened a store with Lizzy's brother-in-law, Samuel R. Perry who had arrived in Fiddletown along with several of Lizzy's siblings. Not mentioned are the three children that Samuel and Lizzy's sister Jane brought with them. Both the Perry family and the Townsends occupied the same building which housed their store and living quarters for each family. Early El Dorado County records assessed Townsend and S.R. Perry for jointly-owned property in 1854.[18] Dennis does not detail the merchandise they offered in their store.

14 *Amador Ledger*, February 16, 1917. Obituary for Elizabeth Townsend, based on her memories of Fiddletown. From the west, the entry to Fiddletown was once through Drytown probably along what is now Quartz Mountain Road.

15 Coburn 178. The express company may have been Byam's Express, which operated out of Fiddletown from 1851-1855. Byam's Express route went from Sacramento (where it connected with Wells Fargo) to the Consumnes River through Cook's Bar, Michigan Bar, then to Fiddletown and Volcano. See also Zorbas, *Fiddletown*, 39 about Byam & Co.'s stage line.

16 Coburn, 46-47.

17 Zorbas, Fiddletown, 22-24, Chapter "Border Town, Tax free Town." The new county of Amador was organized in July 1854, later acquiring a portion that included Fiddletown.

18 El Dorado County *Assessor's Office*, Tax Assessment Role 1854. No property value is given. The 1855 Amador County Tax Assessment roll listed S.R. Perry with a property

California, having no pre-existing supplies, equipment or industry at the time of the Gold Rush, was reliant on obtaining goods such as clothing, dry goods, hardware, foodstuff, liquor, books, and other wares from the East or even other countries. These products were shipped from the eastern states via sea routes to San Francisco and from there by river and pack mules to the gold regions.

Conflicts and Violence

Dennis' letter to Aurelia, written August 31, 1855, covers local and national news. Dennis referred to a contentious State election, where a new political party emerged in 1854. The secretive Know-Nothing party espoused a nationalistic and xenophobic pro-America message that denigrated immigrants and Catholics in reaction to a sizable recent immigration of Irish and German Catholics to the U.S. In the towns and mining camps in California, Know-Nothing proponents targeted foreign miners, especially the Chinese, pressing for their exclusion. Dennis, a man of principle and independent thinking, strongly objected to the Know-Nothing beliefs, affirming that, "When it comes to proscribing a man for his birth or religion I am not in." Nonetheless, this party gained control of the state government in 1855, winning the governorship as well as winning elections in other states in 1854 and 1855.[19]

During the same period in the hot summer of 1855, a different target of intolerance roiled Amador County, greatly affecting its residents. Ethnic hatred against Mexicans and Spanish-speaking Chileans followed savage murders perpetrated in the course of an evening robbery on August 6, 1855 in the small mostly Mexican mining encampment of Lower Rancheria, two miles east of Drytown, not far from Fiddletown.[20] A group of men brandishing guns and knives burst into the community's hotel and store,

value of $550, but he was not included in the 1856 tax assessment roll. The partnership between Dennis and Samuel Perry did not last. He is mentioned in only one more letter. The Census of 1850 and 1860 lists three children living with Samuel R. Perry and wife, Jane. By the 1860 Census, the Perry family had relocated to Rio Vista, Solano County, California.

19 Rolle, Andrew W. *California: A History*, 6th ed. (Wheeling, Ill., Harlan Davidson, Inc., 2003), 162 and Walton E. Bean, *California: An Interpretive History*, 2nd edition (Berkeley, University of California, 1973), 174.

20 [Mason, Jesse D.] *History of Amador County, California, with Illustrations and Biographical Sketches of its Prominent Men and Pioneers* (Oakland, Thompson & West, 1881), 83-88 and Cenotto, *Logan's Alley*, Vol. I, 164-174 devote many pages describing the Rancheria Massacre and the aftermath.

indiscriminately killing the store clerk and owner (who was first wounded with an ax), two card playing hotel customers, a sleeping Indian man and the hotelkeeper's wife as she tried to escape. The murderers stole money and valuables from both buildings. Without proof, Mexicans were accused of the massacre. The following day, a mob rounded up a group of Mexicans living in Rancheria, lynching three men after a quick trial. The violent men who committed the crime remained at large, with fear in the community running high.

Animosity towards Mexicans by white Americans lingered long after the conclusion of Mexican-American War in 1848, in which the U.S. won large areas of territory including California. Mexicans, mostly from Sonora, were early arrivals in the mining regions, perceived by Americans as unwelcome competitors for gold. Tales of Mexican banditry, spurred by stories about Joaquin Murrieta and rumors of reported incidents in nearby mining camps, set the stage for resentment and fear against Mexicans. Passed in 1850, the Foreign Miner's Tax levied a $20 month on foreign miners, mostly affecting the Mexican, Chilean and French populations. Although rescinded the following year, hostility continued to flare between Mexicans and Americans.[21]

Retribution for this brutal crime, known as the Rancheria Massacre, resulted in a month-long siege of violence that exceeded the brutality of the original crime. Mexican and Chilean people, mostly innocent, became targets—many lynched, and all expelled from the county: men, women and children. During this notorious episode at least twenty-four Hispanics were lynched, the Chilean Catholic Church in Drytown was destroyed by arson, and as Dennis described, Spanish speaking people fled the County. This rampage became one of the very worst incidents of lynching and mob violence perpetrated during the lawlessness during and after the Gold Rush.

However, not everybody was taken in by the prevailing anti-Mexican hysteria in Amador County. Dennis' letter written that month to Aurelia, vividly described the panic throughout the Amador County and the horrific impact on local and Hispanic residents. Lorena Hays, living in rural Ione, was affected as well, writing about the crime and its effects in her diary. Both Lorena and Dennis suspected white vigilantes were behind some of the outrages. Lorena observed:

" –murders have taken place, roberies [robberies] committed – in return
men supposed to be the perpetuators have been hung without trial –

---

21 Johnson, Susan Lee, *Roaring Camp: The Social World of the California Gold Rush* (New York, W.W. Norton & Company, 2000), 29-60, 208-212.

peaceful inhabitants driven from their homes, their property destroyed houses and church burned – vigilance committees have been established, companies sent-out and guards stationed in the towns....

Vigilance committees and not violence becoming detestation to the sober & reservable [reserved] part of the community. We fear a great deal more disturbance from these committees and white greasers than from the Mexicans who have been driven from their homes.[22]

Lorena added, "I am weary and heartsick of hearing of so many murders and crimes as are committed daily in our land—but as if there were not enough we must be wearied and disgusted by the disgraceful conduct of men calling themselves law-abiding and civilized inhabitants."

Dennis attributed most murders taking place in the county to brawls, drunkenness and gambling. For instance, the local newspaper described a quarrel at the Union Hotel in Volcano where one man stabbed the other with a large butcher knife, inflicting five wounds. The wounded man died and the Sheriff arrested and jailed the assailant, regarded by the press as a triumph of law and order over lynching.[23] Dennis reported another murder a close to his house in his February 28, 1856 letter. Yet despite the dangers, he assured Aurelia in Christmas of that year they were safe and that civilization was coming to Fiddletown with the arrival of more families, church services and school.

Dennis' letters often referred to the frequency of services at the Methodist Church in Fiddletown as an indication of civilization. What was meant by civilization? To people like the Dennis and Lorena, representing the prevailing values and attitudes of middle-class Protestants, it encompassed propriety, sobriety, following the law in spirit and action, intellectual pursuits, education, and religious observance.[24] And civility! Dennis often contrasted the refinement of New England life to evolving society in Fiddletown, carefully weighing the pros and cons of living in California.

22 Watson, *Hays*, 259-261, August 13, and August 31, 1855. See also editor's comments and notes, pgs. 221-222, 392-3, 413-414.
23 *Volcano Weekly Ledger*, 2, January 12, 1856. The newspaper covered this incident for many weeks especially after the accused man escaped from jail. The murderer, Nathan Cottle, was later tried and sentenced to hang that December.
24 Johnson, Chapter 3, 141-183. Although some regarded the presence of women as a civilizing force, this chapter delves into what constituted "good society," exploring preconceptions and gender relations between the different ethnic groups.

Business, Education and Opportunity

In a January 30, 1856 letter, Dennis again tallied the businesses in Fiddletown: Five taverns, two bakeries, ten stores, three blacksmiths' shops, one jewelry shop, two or three carpentry shops in addition to the church and schoolhouse. [25] The number of stores had decreased by five from his 1853 count; the number of blacksmiths shops and bakeries remained the same, with one more tavern than previously and two more carpenter shops. Had commercial activity decreased in Fiddletown? At most, the population during this decade reached 2,000 inhabitants. Two daily stage lines traveled between Sacramento and Fiddletown, indicating frequent business between the city and foothill mining communities. Dennis reported that Dry Creek, which had previously yielded several fortunes earlier in the Gold Rush, now needed to be worked over two or three times by miners, for less remuneration.

Dennis wrote that he owned a store and several houses, but existing records for the 1856 year do not verify this claim. Dennis and Lizzy owned the building that served as both Post Office and their home on the north side of Fiddletown's Main Street.[26] Deeds for the Fiddletown town site issued in 1871 show that the Townsends owned a single property—lot 13, block 6 on Main Street. Not long after the Townsends arrived in Fiddletown, early records list that Dennis had filed a preemption claim on 160 acres in Loafer's Flat, a promising mining area about half mile southwest of Fiddletown.[27] Apparently he never took the steps to improve the land, so he must have not finalized purchase of the property.

By the end of 1855 through the end of 1856 Dennis pursued several enterprises in addition to being Postmaster. He continued to manage a store, this time on his own. The store held a large inventory of newspapers from various cities in the East, South and California, described in letters sent

25 Meacham, Chronicle, 17 and [card] Index to the Townsend Papers: Dennis Townsend. This letter, written by Dennis to his parents, is missing, summarized by Meacham.

26 Amador County, *Tax Assessment Roll*, 1855 and 1856. Dennis Townsend was listed with improvements and personal property totaling $600. Dennis' letter to Aurelia on December 24, 1856 includes a floor plan of his combined home and Post Office. Assessment records for Amador County are very sporadic, leaving gaps in information. They are available in the Amador County Archives for only 1855, 1856, 1878-9, and 1892.

27 El Dorado County *Preemption Book* [circa 1853], no. 217. The Preemption Act of 1841 gave settlers a right to purchase public land at a federal minimal price if steps were taken to develop and improve the land.

to Aurelia on December 3, 1855 and February 28, 1856. The newspapers reflected the origins of the town's American population, originating from many states of the Union. With available newspapers, Dennis could also keep up with national and state news. The Boston newspaper carried in his repertoire covered the city where his eldest brother Elmer lived; the New Orleans newspaper covered Louisiana where Alfred resided. Dennis sold over 60 California newspapers, including a newspaper written in Spanish. He kept in stock a selection of stationery, essential during those times when business and personal correspondence was written by hand. In addition, his store offered a small choice of books for sale and featured a circulating library where residents could borrow books—the first in Fiddletown. He expanded his wares to in 1856 to include a variety of musical instruments, itemized in a letter to his parents written on April 18, 1856. In response to the presence of families in Fiddletown, Dennis even stocked toys for children during the Christmas holidays. A similar enterprise in 1856 in the town of Volcano furnished newspapers, magazines, stationery and books. That business also sold school books, cigars and tobacco.[28]

Dennis ultimately made his reputation as a teacher, yet almost as an aside, his December 3, 1855 letter mentioned that he was teaching school for three months at $80/month. Locally organized common schools, which had proliferated in the 1830s across other sections of the country, started cropping up in the gold mining regions with the settlement of towns. As early as 1853, Volcano as well as Drytown, Jackson, Sutter Creek and Ione established schools in Amador County, some located in church buildings. Fiddletown's first one-room schoolhouse was built in 1855 at the corner of Church and Main Street.

Dennis Townsend is credited as being Fiddletown's first schoolteacher by Jesse D. Mason, Amador County's first historian and a resident of the county. [29] But the following year in his letter of December 24, 1856, Dennis mentioned that another teacher named Kemp from Massachusetts taught in the school. However, by February 1857, Dennis was back teaching, apparently by popular demand. Yet, it was not his primary occupation, especially since the school session was short.

At the time, California schools were mandated by the state constitution to be open at least three months a year and supported by the sale of public

28 Cenotto, Vol. II, 40. George Johnson & Co. advertised their business in the *Volcano Ledger* in 1857 as the "Volcano News Depot," and the "Volcano Literary Depot."
29 Mason, 225. See also *Logan's Alley*, Vol. III, 53, footnote: Jesse D. Mason was a resident of Amador County from the early 1850s through 1877, the same period that the Townsends were there. He lived in Volcano from 1853-58.

lands. A school session of three months was common throughout the country, usually following the farm schedule with sessions in the winter and sometimes summer. Spring planting and fall harvest times were busy in rural areas. Most common schools taught the basics of reading, writing, and arithmetic, with an emphasis on memorization and oratory. Teachers were often young and inexperienced, and many did not stay long. Initially, they were mostly male. The low wages and the short sessions forced teachers to take on other jobs.[30] Although educated and experienced, Dennis, like other teachers, wore many hats in order to make a living.

Dennis had written little about the job of being Postmaster since his appointment, other than references in his letter of December 3, 1855 regarding the safety of U.S. Mail and faster delivery to California from the East compared to the South. In January, 1855, steamship delivery of the mail was improved by the completion of a railroad in Panama that went from Chagres to Panama City, shortening a trip by canoe and mule that took at least five days. In addition to mail delivery by steamship, overland routes to California via Salt Lake City had been established as early as 1851, initially encountering obstacles with Indian attacks and inclement weather. New routes followed the Mormon Trail but attempted to avoid the Sierra Nevada Mountains. From 1854-1858, mail was carried by horseback, pack mules or wagons from Salt Lake City to San Francisco, and south from there by steamship. Delivery time by steamship coast to coast took 18 to 22 days in contrast to 23 to 25 days by stagecoach to St. Louis.[31]

Mail destined for gold rush towns still arrived by steamship to San Francisco, distributed from there to post offices in the Sierra Nevada foothills which must have taken a day or two. Dennis' position as Fiddletown Postmaster became progressively more demanding as expressed in his 1856 letters. In a letter written on December 24, 1856, Dennis revealed his reliance on Pacific Mail Steamship's twice monthly scheduled arrivals and departures. By the time mail arrived in Fiddletown, Dennis had to rush to process incoming letters and parcels while preparing and collecting outgoing mail for the next sailing several days later. He became increasingly harried as Postmaster, under pressure to get the mail out before the San Francisco departure of the Pacific Mail Steamship carrying letters destined for the East and other regions of the country.

---

30 Kastle, Carl E. *Pillars of the Republic: Common Schools and American Society,* 1780-1960 (New York, Hill & Wang, 1983) 13-21.

31 Coburn 107-110, and United Stated Postal Service: about.usps.com/who/profile/ history/overland-mail.htm.

After three letters written in 1856, his correspondence to his family dropped off with only one short letter to sister Susan composed in 1857, a short letter to Aurelia in 1858 and no letters written in 1859. On November 27, 1857, the Townsend's daughter, Mary Emma, was born—mentioned five months later in the 1858 letter. The joy of parenthood became another factor that preoccupied Dennis and Lizzy.

Busy as he was, Dennis developed his many interests: photography, music, and agriculture. His letters to his parents of April 18, 1856 and Aurelia (May 1, 1858 and February 17, 1860) reveal his talents and skills. These letters plus a lengthy letter written to Aurelia on February 17, 1860 refer to these activities.

In the mid-19th century, the phonograph and other means to record music had not been invented. As in centuries past, the performance of music occurred in people's homes, in churches, in public places, in schools. Dennis had learned to play the violin as a young man. In California, he not only sold violins, but he assured his parents that his playing had improved. He also dabbled in the guitar. As early as 1854, he purchased a melodeon for Lizzy and in 1860, referred to acquiring another one. In spare moments, he studied how to play this keyboard instrument, much like a harmonium. During his time in Fiddletown Dennis served as a singing master, teaching several singing schools over the years.[32] In February, 1860, in addition teaching singing school, he led the choir at the Methodist Church in Fiddletown. Dennis must have had a fine singing voice and his musical abilities added to the reputation of a town where people were known playing the fiddle and perhaps for fiddling around.[33]

The California Gold Rush drew professional and amateur photographers alike. All were eager to document miners and the emerging mining towns that sprung from the wilderness. Daguerreotype photography involved many steps of preparation including polishing and treating a silver-plated copper plate, exposing it to light in a camera from one to thirty seconds, then developing the plate with vapor from heated mercury, and finally fixing and enhancing the image with other chemicals. [34] Dennis continued

32 https://www.loc.gov/collections/music-of-nineteenth-century-ohio/articles-and-essays/singing-schools. Singing schools taught basic music sight reading and the mechanics of singing. Popular in New England, they were connected with congregational singing in Protestant churches.

33 Zorbas, *Fiddletown*, 19-21, "How Fiddletown Got its Name."

34 Aspinwall, Jane L. *Golden Prospects: of the California Gold Rush*, (Hall Family Foundation in Association with the Nelson Atkins Museum of Art, Kansas City, Missouri, 2019), 10. See Chapters 3 and 4 regarding photography in the gold regions and towns. Miners commemorated their participation in the Gold Rush with portraits;

to be fascinated with daguerreotype photography, which he previously practiced in Illinois. He yearned for members of his family to send him their portraits. He had taken a photograph of Volcano when he arrived there, and in Fiddletown he continued to take photographs of the town and people. A few that survived are reproduced in this book.

Townsend's daguerreotype of Fiddletown, accompanying his September 17, 1857 letter to Susan, depicts the northeastern commercial portion of Main Street, displaying the front of Post Office where he and Lizzy lived and worked (the third structure portrayed).[35] The building in the forefront, Belle Creole Baths, reveals that public baths were available in town. The *Water-Cure Journal*, read by Lorena, sister Eliza and referred to by Dennis, advocated hydrotherapy or the "water-cure," a method to treat health problems, particularly those of women, but also followed by men. Water-cure establishments were staffed by women for women.[36] Could Belle Creole Baths Fiddletown have offered such services?

In his February 17, 1860 letter, to Aurelia, Dennis revealed that he had resumed taking daguerreotype photographs as a business, sacrificing his teaching job. However, he was not successful monetarily. Yet in the nearby Amador County town of Ione, Elizabeth Withington, a woman, wife, mother and photographer, established a successful photography business in 1857. Advertising her services in the *Amador Weekly Ledger* of October 3, 1857, she set up a dedicated photography studio for taking photographs of local people. Withington's business flourished for decades as she kept up with changing techniques and trends.[37] Undoubtedly, she had skills in marketing, a quality that evaded Dennis when he embarked much later on a new enterprise.

During his time in Fiddletown, Dennis never lost his interest in agriculture. Not only did he send seeds to his parents, but he told Aurelia in this same February letter that he found land by the creek where he intended to grow vegetables. Gardening was the closest he got to farming.

business owners and merchants displayed success with photographs of their buildings.
35 Aspinwall, 92 and Zorbas, *Fiddletown*, 7, reproduce an early 1850 photograph labeled as Fiddletown taken by an unknown photographer. Townsend's photograph is the only authenticated photograph of the town in the 1850s.
36 Watson, *Hays*, 235, 242, January 22, 1854 and May 27, 1854. See Watson's editorial comments, 214, about this popular health reform of the Victorian era [to] treat diseases.
37 Maxell, Anne, *Women Photographers of the Pacific World, 1857-1930*. (New York, Routledge, 2020). See "Elizabeth Withington, Pioneering Professionalism," 29-48. In the 1870s, Withington gravitated from portraiture to landscape photography, taking stereographs of scenes and landmarks in the nearby Sierra Nevada. These stereographs are in the collection of the Amador County Archives. See also Watson *Hays*, 225-6.

In these first years in California, Dennis had enjoyed good health, the mild climate, and new opportunities. He cobbled several jobs together to earn a living, while pursuing creative endeavors with music and photography. As the owner of a store stocking newspapers and books, and also as a part-time teacher, he did much to further education and reading in the Fiddletown area. Ever since his arrival there, Dennis evaluated living in California, which he grew to like more and more. So far California had been good to him and he intended to stay permanently. The remainder of the 1860s would bring new challenges.

Letters: 1853 - 1860

Fiddletown, Apr. 11th, 1853

Dear Sister Aurelia[1],

    I have received a letter catalogue from you recently. I rejoice at the indications of your prosperity in the catalogue and thank you sincerely in my heart, for your good letter. I have mined until recently say two weeks ago when we came to Fiddletown. Two young men and myself have rented a house at 100$ per month and opened a tavern[2] in connection with a small store. We rented the house for one month with the refusal of it for any number of months not exceeding six months. Don't know how the concern will pay eventually, but we are getting a good run of customers at present. Fiddletown is a very wicked place though they have preaching here every Sunday. Frequent cases of murder and robbery occur in this vicinity. This place is about 50 miles from Sacramento City. As there is no post office in this place I wish you to direct to Sacramento City and we can easily get your letters by express. We keep an express office and run a team weekly to the city.[3] I have just rec'd a letter from Alfred dated Jan. 1st ; he wishes me to join him in business and says that I can do better with him unless I am doing astonishingly well where I am.[4] I would rather that he would open a store in Cal—as I think the climate is much more healthy than that of any other state in the union and there are excellent chances for making money here in trade. Whatever Alfred and I determine on is for the best I shall do. I saved

---

1 Sister, Aurelia was married Reverend Horace Herrick in 1835. In the 1840s, they were living in Fitzwilliam, New Hampshire,

2 Doble, 34. John Doble mentioned going a store, boarding house and tavern together on a main road. https://en.wikipedia.org/wiki/Tavern. "Over time the words 'tavern' and 'inn' became synonymous." In this case, the tavern was a place where travelers could lodge and obtain food and possibly drink with an adjoining store.

3 Coburn, *Letters of* Gold, 150-153 and J.S. Holliday, *Rush for Riches: Gold Fever and the Making of California* (Oakland Museum of California and the University of California Press, 1999), 28-131.Express mail companies arose as early as 1849 to satisfy the pressing desire of miners for correspondence with families, news of the world, business correspondence and transportation of gold dust. Mail from surrounding mining camps were picked up and delivered to express offices in supply towns such as Fiddletown.

4 Alfred was in Texas in 1852, moving the next year to set up business in Vienna, Louisiana. It took his letter four months to arrive in Fiddletown.

something by mining. Have not time to write more at present. I will write often but will not promise long letters.

Your affectionate Br.

Dennis Townsend

Send our wishes. Brother & Sisters are coming out this season.[5]
Enclosed my wife Lizzy sends you a specimen of the shining dust together with her best respects.[6]

UTAustin/VHS MSC133: 8

---

5 These wishes were squeezed in at the bottom of the letter. The different rounded handwriting indicates that they were likely written by Lizzy whose family left for California the next month.

6 This insert was written at the top of the letter in the left margin. The rounded handwriting was probably from Lizzy.

Fiddletown, May 17th, 1853

Dear Father,

Your letter of March 9th was brought to me from Volcano a few days ago. I rejoice to learn that you are in good health and thank you for your good advice. We are now in a public house, and have been for about two months. I am connected with two young men in the business. We pay 100$ rent for house per month, run a team weekly to Sacramento City and, in connection with a tavern, keep a small stock of goods. Don't know how long we shall continue the business. My lady has a brother-in-law & family, a brother and two sisters now on the "Plains."[7] They started early with horse & mule teams and brought along feed for them. We expect to see them in July. I mined until I left Volcano and saved something but mining has become a very uncertain business. Almost anything else is surer to pay. There has been more rain this spring than is usual for California which is favorable to farmers. The climate is very pleasant and we enjoy good health. Have rec'd no letter from Wm. except one he wrote before our arrival in Ca. Rec'd a letter from Alfred a short time since. He says that he has got well fixed and wishes me to join him in trade which I may do after a while. I think the climate of Ca. would suit him, but I will not advise any brother or sister to come here, for it is a long journey attended with risks and one might not do well after his arrival, though I think there are more and better chances of success here than in any other part of the Union. I have not been out of the mountains since my arrival, but they say that the valleys are most lovely now. Vegetation [is] very luxuriant and [with] the greatest variety and profusion of flowers. It would astonish you to see the vegetables of this country. Their size and excellence are beyond comparison. Turnips, beets, potatoes possess a delicacy of flavor that I never knew in the New England States. Buren spoke to me about a monument that has been erected to our departed relatives. I shall be happy to contribute something after a while, but just now I have need of every dollar in our business. I hope also to be able to send money enough to procure all of your Daguerreotypes, and send you mine and lady's.

I say Lizzy, I mean my wife. Lizzy thinks that you write remarkable well for a man of your age.[8] We hope that years of happiness are yet in store for

---

7 The family of Elizabeth "Lizzy" Ray Townsend, no doubt inspired and encouraged by the successful journey of Lizzy and Dennis, were among the 20,000 emigrants making the overland trip in 1853.

8 William Townsend was 73 years old at this time. He was born in Lynnfield, Mass. in 1780.

you. Remember a letter from you is almost as good as a visit. Orlando Holt is within 30 miles. We have exchanged letters once. He tells me that he is mining. Tell me about your farm stock crop, etc.

Your affectionate son,

Dennis Townsend

Dear Mother— Lizzy was very much pleased with receiving your letter and intended to write to you in this but she cannot find time at present. She is very much hurried with work, as you know she must be in a public house. She will write you the first opportunity.[9]

Affectionately

Dennis Townsend[10]

Dear Brother Van Buren,

It affords me peculiar pleasure to receive and letter from you and Marquis whose handwriting I had never before seen. You say that you would like to dig up the shining dust. Perhaps you may do just as well where you are though you may not make so much money. Money is not worth a quarter as such here as in Vermont, so if you make a quarter as much there as you could here, you are doing just as well not to leave your native state unless it be for the benefit of your health. I will be honest enough however, to acknowledge that I could not be satisfied to spend my days among the rocks and snows of Vermont. I am glad that the legislature of your state has done something to restrain intemperance. California beats all the places for drinking. Buren, I recollect the last that I was at home an accident happened to one of your eyes while you were playing in the street. So you carry the mark yet?

Your Affectionate Brother

Dennis

---

9 This added note was written sideways in the margin on the first page of the letter. Lizzy was also working in the tavern.

10 The letters that follow, addressed to Dennis' siblings were enclosed with the May 17, 1853 letter.

Dear Brother Marquis[11],

You were a little chub of a fellow the last time I saw you, but I suppose I would not know you now. Probably you have altered some but amid all the changes I think you must have a good head left, for I used to think it was a model for the phrenologist. You must be sure to come and see us as soon as the cars[12] commence running. There are thousands of Chinese here. They are a weak and singular race subsisting principally on tea and rice.[13] The Indians seem to have a great deal of antipathy against them and they shoot them when they can do it secretly. One was shot by an Indian today about 3 miles from town. Several murders have been committed in this vicinity recently. Society is not yet thoroughly settled in the mines though it is said to be very good on the coast. I wish you to tell me something about the farm the next time you write. It would make your eyes stick out, I suppose, to be ensured 20 cents per pound for potatoes, 8 cents for turnips & beets, 50 cents for onions, 10 cents for barley & hay which are the prices at present in Fiddletown. A man can make thousands of dollars off from a few acres of ground, here in the mountains but tillable land is very scarce. I don't get time to write much. Tell Alstyne, Torrey and Valette that I will try to favor them with a few lines soon. Don't be too crazy about the girls for a year or two. How old are you?
Your Affectionate Brother

Dennis Townsend

Dear Sister Eliza,[14]

Mother sent us a lock of your hair. I was astonished to discover that it had changed from a bright red to beautiful brown. My Lizzy curls, combs & forwards mine sometimes but when she arrives at the top of my cranium

---

11 Marquis, the baby of the family, was only 5 years old when Dennis left New England. He was now 18 years old.

12 Dennis was referring to trains east of the Mississippi. https://www.american-rails.com/1840s.html. By 1850 railroads had blossomed into a unified matrix with lines linking the east coast and Midwest." The transcontinental railroad leading to California was not completed until 1869.

13 Townsends encountered Chinese for the first time, making the assumption that they were weak because they were not violent. The treatment of Chinese by Indians as described by Dennis is new information for the author.

14 Letter to Eliza was written on same sheet of paper as the previous letter to Marquis.

she finds barren soil that produces no vegetation. Wouldn't there be a motley company of us if we should all get together? but this we cannot reasonably expect in this world though I hope to see all of my brothers and sisters before I die. Tell Father and Mother that we would like to receive a lock of their hair by the next letter.[15] I think that I shall be just as likely to visit Vermont again in a few years as if I were [living] in Illinois or Louisiana. I wrote to Wm when I first arrived but have rec'd no answer. The only way for me to correspond with my parents and all my brothers & sisters is to write short letters. I was a good deal shocked to hear of the death of Cousin James Townsend and Oliver Swain. Life is uncertain and there seems to be but little worth living for except the joys that flow from friendship and the family relations and the proper cultivation of the mind. Society is very good in some parts of Ca. but I cannot say much in favor of Fiddletown. It is true we have a Methodist meeting[16] here occasionally but the preacher is quite ordinary and has but few hearers. The arrival of families has improved the society some of late but still as a general thing the people are very immoral. If we remain in the country we do not intend stopping here long, though all is uncertainty yet. Please direct your letters to Sacramento City until I give you further notice. We may have a Post Office in Fiddletown soon.

Yours Aff'ty

Dennis Townsend

---

15 Locks of hair were sent as tokens of love and affection in Victorian times, before photographs were pervasive.

16 Words smeared, ink spots, writing scrawled indicating Dennis was rushed.

Fiddletown, November 12, 1853

Dear Sister Aurelia,

Your letter has been rec'd and I delay not to reply, though in but a few words. It appears that you had been enjoying yourself with Wealthy Ann[17] and the nieces, and brother Herrick had been on the salt water for his health but it was all over and you had got back to Montpelier into the old school room again after a little journey and visiting home is certainly sweeter than ever. Though I have led a rather unsettled life, home is the sweetest spot that I could ever find. Since I last wrote you my brother-in-law S.R. Perry & family one brother and two sisters of my wife have arrived from the plains.[18] They were very well prepared for the trip and got in safe with the loss of a small portion of their teams. I have taken an interest with my brother-in-law in a store. Times are dull just now on account of a scarcity of water for mining purposes, but the rainy season will probably set in very soon and give a powerful impulse to business. I think that I shall be able to get a good living at any rate. My wife and I have enjoyed remarkable health in this country. You express fears that some fatal accident might befall me in this rude country where vice and crime abound to such an extent, I feel as safe here as anywhere. Safety depends more upon a man's own conduct than the place where [one] lives. The blackest crimes are committed even in the most refined communities. It is my aim to pursue a course that my conscience will approve and leave all contingencies to providence. I am glad to learn that all our friends are doing reasonable well. In the course of a few years if life is spared I may join Alfred. We correspond regularly. Wm seems to be rather mute of late. I rec'd a letter from him when we first arrived here but none since. Hope he is doing well. Don't recollect whether I answered the letter from Norwich. Father and mother write excellent letters and so do the rest. Don't know that I can write anything about the country that you do not get in the papers. The great burden of California news is "<u>Extraordinary</u> diggings, new <u>discoveries</u>, <u>gold taken</u> out by the pound, etc. etc," half of which is fiction got up to draw people to different points for the purpose of getting their money. We expect to have a post office here shortly and I shall act as postmaster.[19] This will draw custom to the house though the per-

---

17 Wealthy Ann Beecher was the wife of oldest brother, Elmer Townsend.

18 The family of Elizabeth "Lizzy" Ray Townsend included her sister Jane, married to Samuel R. Perry, her sister Margaret, later married to Edward Kingsley and her brother, John Ray. Note that only Mr. Perry is named.

19 Coburn, *Letters of Gold* The Fiddletown Post Office was established on December

centage on post office matter will be trifling. Direct [letters] to Sacramento once more, and I expect to be able then to give other directions. I have seen Orlando W. Holt in Coloma [20] He is a very steady industrious man and has saved in the three years that he has been here about three thousand dollars. He thinks of settling in Wisconsin where he has land. I have written to him to visit Fiddletown for winter diggings.

Affectionately

Dennis Townsend[21]

31, 1853.

20 According to the 1850 U.S. Census, Orlando Holt, a Vermont native, was staying in the vicinity of Placerville (Coloma) and residing in a household with twenty people. Holt eventually left California for Wisconsin as he had planned. The 1860 U.S. Census lists him as a farmer in Waterford, Racine County, Wisconsin. Coloma is where gold was discovered, about 27 or so miles north of Fiddletown.

21 The penmanship on this letter is very precise and beautiful, with flourishes and careful wording. The envelope accompanying the letter is addressed to Mrs. Aurelia Herrick, Montpelier, Vermont. At the bottom "curry down the rooster" is written.

Fiddletown Nov 18th 1853

Dear Father,[22]

Your very kind and interesting letters received some weeks since I think I have not answered. I was rejoiced to learn that you were all enjoying good health and comfortably situated. Time passes and marks his change upon us all. When I look back to boyhood I think of my little self, trotting upon your knee at the tune of "Peggy and Molly." Again I shoot my little cross gun; run out again to <u>Putty Cats house</u> and build barns and fill them with hay and brush cattle while I see brothers and sisters around me and father and mother strugling [struggling] to maintain a numerous family. Everything about the old place is clear to my mind's eye, every not [knot] hole in the old barn, the wall around the yard capped with hewn logs, the goose pond where I have spent many an hour singing with the frogs, or busied with my water wheels, the tall trees around the farm on which the hawks and crows perched, which seldom remained until I could get near them with the old musket, the neighboring farms and buildings around, Ascutney[23] in the distance in fair weather looming high into the clear blue sky or snow capped with lowering clouds when storms were near. These are a few objects associated with my early hopes and feelings when imagination pictured a thousand bright things for the future but few of which have been realized. Time is hurrying us on through life and soon our places will be filled by others and I do not have reason to be dissatisfied that Providence has ordained it thus. I think it is foolish for a man to deprive himself of the comforts of life and wear himself out in a struggle for wealth that he can never enjoy. It is better to make the best of life we can as it passes; indulge in nothing wrong and at its close we shall be willing to sink to rest as a weary man resigns himself to sleep.

Some of my wife's friends crossed the plains this year. I am now in a store with Perry, my brother-in-law. Our prospects are fair. I design joining Alfred at a future day if circumstances should be favorable. Mr. Perry and family and myself and wife live in the same building but each family has separate apartments and domestic arrangements. Our store is in the same building. We have had some rain and from appearances I judge steady winter rains will set in shortly. The rainy season is the time for business in the

---

22 This letter was written on the same sheet of paper as the next letter to Mother, Susan & Eliza.

23 https://www.vtstateparks.com/ascutney.html. Mt. Ascutney in Vermont has long been a popular hiking destination and was visible from the Townsend farm in Felchville.

mines. There is not much land about Fiddletown fit for cultivation but there are some very rich spots which produce excellent vegetables and men who cultivate them make money rapidly. I rec'd a letter from Buren & Velette not long since which I answered. It appears that the "second crop" are all like to do well.[24] I suppose I have passed the place where you live many a time but I cannot locate it exactly.[25] I have kind of a faint recollection that it is a pretty rough country about there any how. I have not been out of the mining district since we arrived in California. Direct once more to Sacramento and after that I hope we shall have a post office here. We expect a return from our petition from Washington every mail. I expect the appointment of post master.

Your Affectionate Son

Dennis Townsend

VHS MSC133: 7

---

24 This refers to the Townsend children born to Hannah G. Bigelow, Dennis' step-mother.

25 Meacham, 7. Dennis' parents, William and Hannah Bigelow Townsend moved a few miles away from Norwich in 1845 to a place now called New Boston.

[Fiddletown, November 18, 1853][26]

Dear Mother, Susan & Eliza

I hardly know what to write to you except to pass the usual compliments. Several families have moved into Fiddletown this season. Society is improving, less rowdy than formerly. This town and vicinity contain about 1500 inhabitants. There is a steam sawmill here running day and night,[27] three blacksmiths shops, one carpenter's shop, four taverns, two bakeries, two or three restaurants and 15 or 20 stores of different kinds.[28] We have preaching at the Methodist Church every two weeks. The ladies are talking of getting up a fair to repair the church. Balls are quite frequent here. Ascend the hill back of our house and you will look upon a succession of ridges all around you covered thinly with the pine and oak. One mile from town, a few weeks since a man while loafing had the good fortune to pick up a lump of gold worth about 340 dollars. Near the same place a man struck his pick into the seam of rock which opened and exhibited a perfect landscape picture upon the inner face of the rock, trees and shrubs as perfect as any daguerreotype. It was quite a curiosity. In an adjoining county Calaveras the papers give accounts of a wonderful cave recently discovered. There are several apartments. In one about 300 feet below the surface the bones of many people were found many in a state of petrification.[29] New wonders are constantly showing themselves in California. The Indians had no knowledge of this cave and it is thought that the bones belonged to another race anciently inhabiting the country. I have seen Orlando Holt in Coloma. He has made money in this country and seems to be a very moral steady young man. He thinks of returning east and settling in Wisconsin. Perhaps it seems singular to you to talk of going east to Wisconsin. Here we become as familiar with Chinamen as with any other people. Sometimes we see them fresh from

26 This letter was written same sheet of paper as his November 18 letter to Father, which was dated.

27 Zorbas, *Fiddletown*, 10-11. The sawmill owned by McLeod & Farnham must have resumed operation after a terrible boiler explosion in April 1853 that killed Mr. McLeod and badly injured two others.

28 Doble,156. May 13, 1853. By contrast, Doble described Volcano as having 11 stores, 1 restaurant, 3 bakeries, 6 hotels, 3 private boarding houses, 3 bars, 2 gambling houses and an apothecary shop

29 *Sacramento Daily Union,* November 1, 1853 describes discovery of a large and deep cave in Vallecito, Calaveras County in which over 300 petrified human bodies were found, now known as *Moaning Caverns* near Angel's Camp. https://moaningcaverns.com.

China with all their national peculiarities of dress, etc. but soon they adopt American customs in dress especially since in diet to a certain extent many of them live almost entirely upon rice. They are great tea drinkers as you must naturally suppose. We trade with men of all nations including Indians, Negroes, Chinese and Mexicans. There is a right smart sprinkling of French here. My wife wishes to be affectionately remembered to you all. Wishing you long life prosperity and happiness I close.[30]

Very affectionately yours

Dennis Townsend

VHS MSC133: 7

---

30 Dennis' handwriting in this letter is embellished and full of flourishes with a large signature.

Fiddletown Cal., March 8th 1854

Dear Parents Brs. & Sistrs

    If a short letter will do you any good here you have it though I wrote you last some months ago. Health is good, business tolerable, living comfortably and making money slowly. Hope you are all doing well. Business has been very dull through the winter for want of water for gold washing. Did you receive the modle [model] of a <u>tom</u> made of pasteboard from my wife about a year ago?[31] The tom is an instrument used in washing gold. Father, I often think of the cold rocky bleak hill you inhabit buried in snow 3 or 4 months of the year and feel quite uncomfortable at the thought. Here it is very different no snow or cold weather except far up in the mountains, but it matters little about the place where we live provided we are comfortable and contented which I trust you are. The idea of digging and chaffing among the rocks of where you live for a living I must confess, is rather repulsive though it must be admitted that Vermonters manage to live as well as other folks and provide themselves with as many comforts and enjoyment both of body and mind. I wish you all well hoping to get a letter from you soon.
    Affectionately,

Dennis Townsend

VHS MSC133: 7

---

31 This letter reveals that Lizzy's model of the mining tom was made of pasteboard.

Fiddletown Cal February 24, 1855

Dear Father & Mother,

On the other side of this sheet you will find a map of Cal. It is undoubtedly imperfect but better than no map at all. If you look sharp you will discover the position of Fiddletown which is about 50 miles from Sacramento.
This winter has been so remarkably dry that very little mining has been
done in the vicinity of Fiddletown and consequently business has been very
dull. However I have been able to make something. My prospects are favorable for the future in relation to accumulating something for a "rainy day"
and I have never enjoyed better health in any country. My wife is well and
sends her love. Please excuse me for I am in haste.

Your affectionate son

Dennis Townsend

Accompanying this I send a variety of letter sheets[32] for you all at home
parents, brothers and sisters.

UTAustin/VHS MSC133: 8

---

32 Holliday, *Rush for Riches*, 163 and http://www.malakoff.com/goldcountry/capiclet.
htm. Pictorial letter-sheets showing the wonders of California, views of towns, mining
activities, sensational events, etc. were produced in the thousands during the 1850s and
1860s. They featured engravings by artists or daguerreotypes reproduced on writing
paper with space for correspondence. Single sheets could be folded into an envelope
and mailed for forty cents, the minimum postal charge.

Fiddletown Amador Co. Cal Aug.31ˢᵗ 1855

Dear Sister Aurelia,[33]

I rec'd your letter by last mail and was glad to learn that you were so pleasantly situated. I hope Br. Herrick [Horace Herrick, Aurelia's husband] will enjoy better health at his present employment than in teaching. Father and mother wrote me quite a lengthy letter not long since. It does me vast good to get a letter from them, mother is so particular in writing all the news. She tells me all about my old acquaintances. The last letter I rec'd from William informed me that he was preaching to the blacks. I suppose he is trying to tread the path of duty. I have not rec'd any letters from Alfred for a long time. In his last he expressed a desire that I should join him in business, but I was so situated here that it was not advisable for me to leave and such is my situation now. I would like to be with him very much as he needs some healthy person with him to perform the heavy labor of his business.[34] Times are very dull through the dry season but I am so situated as to make something all of the time though nothing great.

Politicks [politics] run pretty high just at this time as our State election comes off in about a week. I am no politician though I have hitherto voted with the Whigs, but the Know Nothing creed I can't begin to swallow. When it comes to proscribing a man for his birth or religion I am not in. I have frequently sent papers [newspapers] to my friends in different places. Alstyne [brother] and Father have acknowledged rec't of them but I don't know whether the rest of you get them or not.

I send Brother Herrick by this mail $30 in gold coin, a Twenty and a Ten Dollar piece enclosed in a miniature case, thinking this conveyance as safe as any. It is directed to Mr. Horace Herrick, 69 Hanover Street, Boston Mass. I make him this return for the favor he did me 13 years ago and am greatly obliged to him besides. If he gets it please acknowledge rec't by return of mail.

My wife has now in Cal. a brother and two sisters which renders her residence here considerably home like. Though she was always satisfied before they came; she thinks a woman is a poor excuse who can't be contented with her husband.[35] It has been a fearful time with us recently

---

33 This letter was written on four pages.

34 Townsend, F.T. *Autobiography*, 16. Alfred was in the mercantile business.

35 This implies some conflict between the Jane and Samuel Perry. It is the last time Dennis refers to this family. Samuel R. Perry sued members of the Consumnes Mining & Ditching Company on December 12, 1855 for not repaying debt he bore for another

and so it is now. Two or three weeks ago a guerrilla party of Mexicans entered a small mining village (Rancheria) about 6 miles from here about 9 o'clock at night, slaughtered six men and one lady, got 6[000] or $8000 and fled. Besides this <u>single [incident]</u>, murders and robberies are frequent. The whites in some instances armed the Indians and told them to kill all the Mexicans they could. They picked off several, doubtless some who were innocent. The Sheriff of our county with a posse went in pursuit of the first named party. Came up with some of them, had an encounter in which the sheriff was killed and a Mexican or two. The Mexicans fought desperately each with two revolvers, one in each hand. It is supposed that the party have all or nearly all now suffered the penalty due their crime. When the whites got hold of one, they held an expeditious trial and if he was convicted they dragged him up the nearest limb without further ceremony. We have a guard out every night in Fiddletown. The people of the county have passed resolutions banishing all <u>suspicious</u> Mexicans from the county and disarming <u>all</u>. It is thought by many that white men are at the head of these Mexican desperados and instigate them to their bloody deeds. The last act prohibiting gambling in this state has turned many an idler out to highway robbery and theft. It is dangerous for a man to travel alone in this vicinity. A man was robbed a mile [or] two from here a few days since. Hope this state of things will not continue long. We have at present two daily lines of stages from Sacramento through to this place.

I break off short here.

Your Afft' Brother

Dennis Townsend

We would very much like to receive Bro Herrick's and your Daguerreotypes.[36]

UTAustin/ VHS MSC133: 8

party. At some point Samuel and Jane and their children relocated to the Rio Vista area in Solano County. The only other reference to Samuel in Amador County records is a September 21, 1877 Judgement in a lawsuit against Mechanics Mining Company that awarded $231.50 indebted to him.

36 This sentence was added.at the top of first page of the letter. Handwriting on the letter becomes scrawled and agitated as it proceeds.

Fiddletown Amador Co Cal Aug. 31st, 1855

Mr. Horace Herick [Herrick]

Dear Brother,

I got a letter from Aurelia by last mail which informed me that [you] were employed in Boston. I was glad to learn that you were both enjoying comfortable health. I and mine are well.   I am very happy to enclose in this $30 (Thirty Dollars) for you in return for the favor you conferred on me upwards of thirteen years ago. Please destroy the note you hold against me for $15 and acknowledge the receipt of this by return of mail.

Ever Yours Affectionately

Dennis Townsend

Fiddletown Amador Co. Cal. Dec. 3 1855

Dear Sister Aurelia,

Your letter I have just rec'd. I have but a few moments to spare before closing the mail. We were much disappointed by not receiving your daguerreotypes as you gave us reason to expect by a letter two weeks ago. I should prefer sending by Mail rather than by express, as it will come directly to here and with quite as good a chance of safety.

[37] As to your dress and fashion of your hair, if you please your own taste you will suit me. However I would like to see you look as you ordinarily do and not as if you had taken particular pains to fix up for a picture. I rec'd a letter from Alfred and one from William by last mail, the same time that I rec'd your last. They were dated one month earlier than yours. So that you perceive, letters come quicker from Boston & New York than from Louisiana. Alfred writes that times are a little close with him in consequence of short crops. He says that their concern had standing out last year about $30,000 and they will have due by the 1st of Jan. $70,000, that they will owe about $35,000 falling due before next Aug. He hopes to collect enough to pay, etc. etc. He is still anxious to locate somewhere in the gulf of Texas on account of his health.[38] Alfred has 3 daughters and one son. His oldest is going to school. Wm. writes that they have seven children including Zeona Charlotte by his first wife and his step-daughter Margaret Louis Harrell.[39] He is very zealous in the cause of the Colored Mission. He has a certain field in his vicinity and preaches to the blacks altogether. Hope he will keep in the path of duty whatever it may be. The paper you sent will probably come day after tomorrow. I send Brother Herrick a Spanish paper by this mail. I deal in papers and receive about one hundred Atlantic papers of different kinds every mail. I also get 60 or 80 California papers every week to supply customers. I have a small stock of books and stationary and keep also a Circulating Library. My little business pays me something besides. I am at present engaged in teaching from which I shall realize about $80 per

37 Coburn, 46-7 Private express mail coexisted with U.S. mail, but was more expensive. Mail through the Postal Service was delivered to San Francisco by the Pacific Mail Steamship Company and from there to the gold country.

38 Meacham, 4, 13-14. As a young man, Alfred came down with "lung fever, which resulted in the collapse of one lung. In 1853, he relocated from Texas to Vienna, Louisiana where he established a business. Before that, he had a farm in Texas where he owned a few black slaves. It appears that he wanted to return to Texas.

39 Meacham, 11. Zeona was seven months old when William's first wife died. A year later, on November 7, 1845 he remarried a widow with a year-old daughter.

month.[40] You ask me why my letters are not franked. It is because the P.O. pays more than $200 per year and the franking privilege[41] is not allowed in such case. Enclosed I send you a few stamps. I wish you to write very often. I have frequently sent papers to my relatives in different places. I sent some to Susan directing them to Susan Fay, South Reading Vermont, is this her address? I am sorry to hear that she is in such bad health.[42] Please write me <u>unreserved</u> about her. I frequently send Orson papers but have got no answer from them nor from those I sent [to] Susan. Excuse me for I have no time to write more. Lizzy joins me in love to you and Mr. Herrick.

Your aft' Br

Dennis Townsend

I send you a Paper by this mail.

UTAustin/VHS MSC133: 8

---

40 Mason, 225 and Zorbas, 67-68. Townsend was identified as the first teacher of Fiddletown School, which opened in 1855.

41 Coburn, 54, 293-325. As of April 1855, all domestic mail had to be prepaid with affixed postal stamps. Postage cost 40 cents for a single letter and 12 ½ cents for intra-California mail and letters between California & Oregon. Post offices had to have an annual revenue of $500 to receive a metal handstamp for making postmarks. The franking privilege, for which outgoing mail could be sent for free, was given to congressmen, some governmental officials and many postmasters. Presumably Dennis' annual salary was deemed sufficient by the Postal Service to deny him the franking privilege.

42 Meacham,15. Susan married Ezra Fay on May 24, 1855. As learned later, she was pregnant, not sick with an illness.

Fiddletown, Amador County, Feb. 28th, 1856

Dear Brother & Sister [Aurelia and Horace Herrick],

Believing that you would prefer receiving a short letter from us to none I now occupy a few moments in writing. I cannot promise to write often unless I write briefly. By the tenure of your last, Aurelia, I judge you consider us surrounded with uncommon dangers. This is not the case at present. I suppose you got the impression from reading accounts of Indian troubles at the north. All is quiet here. It is true murders are frequent here, but they are generally confined to brawling, gambling, drinking naturally thrown together in such a country as this. You ask me if we have snow. I answer no. There has been a little white frost two or three times this winter and I have seen slight scales of ice rarely in the morning, in two or three instances. The weather has been delightful up to the present time—most [mostly] too pleasant for prosperity as there has been but little rain to supply miners with the indispensable element water for gold washing.

By last mail I sent Father a Daguerreotype of Fiddletown taken 18 months ago or more.[43] There have been great improvements in the place since but it will give you an idea of the locality. I sent him the late Governors message,[44] which you will find to be very interesting as it treats quite extensively of the natural advantages and resources of the state. I like Cal. far better than anticipated. I have never enjoyed good health anywhere as here. I don't anticipate making a fortune suddenly but I can easily make a living and gradually accumulate something for a future day. I thank [you] for the papers you sent, but will not give you the trouble to send more unless you find something which you are anxious for me to see. I tell you this as I deal in papers from the different Atlantic states receiving them every mail. At present on each arrival I get about 140. They comprise papers from Boston, New York, Philadelphia, Baltimore, Cincinnati, Louisville, Chicago, Saint Louis and New Orleans, besides these I sell about 200 weekly which are published in this state. With this I send you the pictures taken from two letter sheets. One containing a description of the mammoth forest in an adjoining county, all true to the letter.[45] The other is a daguerreotype view

43 This daguerreotype of Fiddletown has not been found. It is not in the collections of both repositories of the Townsend letters.

44 J. Neely Johnson became California Governor as of January 9, 1856. Townsend may be referring to the previous governor, John Bigler, since his letter to his father was sent at least 18 months before this letter.

45 The Big Trees State Park in Calaveras County contains two groves of giant Sequoias. For letter sheets, see the Bancroft Library's Honeyman collection, the California State

or a copy rather of a Daguerreotype view of a Lynch execution of a Mexican engaged in the Rancheria tragedy last summer.[46] The description is miserably written but I can't help that. Rancheria is distant from this town about 4 miles. A murder was committed a few doors from mine last week resulting from drinking and gambling. One German stabbed another. The criminal is now in jail awaiting his trial.[47]

I am obliged now to close.

Yours Affectionately

Dennis Townsend

Library, etc.

46 Cenotto, vol. I, 171-2. Rafael Escobar was seized from the Sheriff on August 15 1855, and lynched by a mob on the hanging tree in central Jackson, the county seat. He was the tenth and last person (not all connected with Rancheria) to be lynched on this tree, but not the last lynched in retribution for the murders in Rancheria.

47 *Volcano Weekly Ledger*, June 28, 1856. The District Court trial concluded with a verdict of manslaughter instead of murder.

Fiddletown Amador Co Cal Apr 18th, 1856

Dear Parents,

Yours of Mar 7th acknowledging rec't of Daguerreotype of Fiddletown is rec'd. In answer to your inquiry about the trees shown in the picture, I would say that the tree in the centre of the town is a large oak but nothing wonderful in size. The trees in the back ground are pines. As you manifest some interest in the mammoth trees of Cal. I send you this sheet which gives a true description of a forest twenty or thirty miles from this place in an adjoining county. Father, I sent you a few kernels of wheat, barley and wild oats[48] about a month ago, which appears you had not received when you wrote. Hope you have received them ere this. I have a large mail to make up tonight so that I am forced to write briefly and in haste. Lizzy has not time to write now. It gives us both great pleasure to receive letters from you. You ask me mother, if I play upon the violin as I used to. Yes but I think I have improved some. I bought a melodeon[49] for my wife 18 months ago. She plays some tunes. I play the guitar a <u>little</u>. I keep for sale flutes, violins, guitars, banjos tamborines [tambourines] and accordions.

I was glad Father, to get so <u>long</u> a letter from you. The hog you spoke of must certainly been a great curiosity, but nothing to our grizzly bears which often weigh <u>sixteen</u> <u>hundred</u> [pounds]. They are awful animals, very dangerous. Last week there was a fight in Sacramento between a grizzly and a bull—but such barbarous amusements, I think will soon be put down in this country.[50] Write often if but a few words.

Your Affectionate Son

Dennis Townsend

I think Lizzy will write next mail. You are aware that we get a mail only twice a month.

Love to All

---

48 Zorbas, 62. These staples were the major crops in 1860 Amador County along with potatoes.

49 The melodeon is an upright keyboard instrument sounded with the vibration of free reeds by wind. This American development of the harmonium was quite popular in the 19th century.

50 Pitting a bull against a bear was a gruesome entertainment during and after the California Gold Rush.

Fiddletown, December 24th, 1856

Dear Sister,[51]

Yours of Nov 16 was recd too late to be answered by return mail. The mail steamers usually reach San Francisco about the 1st and 15th of each month and leave on the 8th and 20th so that a person has time to answer letters by return mail though living in the interior of the state, except when the arrival of the boat is unusually late, which was the case the last time.[52] Christmas is immediately upon us. I have just got up a lot of toys for the holidays and the little boys and girls are in ecstasies. They give me not a minute's peace. There is a swarm of boys this moment in my shop amusing themselves with their tin guns. The triggers are clicking and arrows flying about my ears incessantly. I begin to think Fiddletown really _is_ a dangerous place and if I escape being shot it will be by a miracle. Several families have moved in lately and there is a school now in operation numbering upwards of thirty scholars. A young man from Charlestown Mass. by the name of Kemp is teaching. We have preaching two Sundays in a month, such as it is; we also have a singing school now in full blast. In fact the people are becoming somewhat _civilized_ to say the least. Your friend the returned Californian is right about the dangers incident to a connection with gamblers, rowdys [rowdies] and drunkards. I lay claim to no extravagant holiness, but I can say in truth that I never bet a dollar in my life; the extent of my gambling was playing pins in an old wool hat, when a school boy. I was never in a mob, and was never drunk. I abstain from spirituous liquors entirely and have not drunk any tea or coffee since last September. However I claim no credit for abstinence from the last named articles as their excessive use was killing me with the piles.

The situation of your boarding place I think must be very pleasant from the picture you sent. My building is 32 feet square including dwelling and Post Office. It is on the north side of the street the creek [Dry Creek] running back of the yard. The Post Office on the south east corner is 20 feet square. The parlor on the south west is 12 feet front running back 20 feet. Back of this is a room [sitting room] 9' by 18' lying east and west, three feet being occupied between the two rooms by stairway & closets. On the north east corner is the kitchen 14' by 12'. The rooms on the lower floor are all 11

---

51 Meacham, 18.This letter was likely written to Aurelia, who had moved with her husband to live in a boarding house in Montpelier, Vermont.

52 Coburn, 89-90, 107-110; See also Chapter 3 regarding the Pacific Mail Steamship Company.

feet high.[53] If you can understand anything by this diagram please do so.[54] I have mapped it in haste and have not made the relative proportions correctly. Upstairs over the sitting room are two bed rooms and in front, over the parlor and part of the post office is a room,18 by 23 feet unfinished. All the rooms are papered. The front of my post office is nearly all glass.

Feb 3, 1857[55]

Positively I must not undertake to write long letters as I shall never finish them. Since writing the foregoing they have got me into the school house again. It appears that I am the only man they can get to suit them but I don't know as I shall teach longer than 3 months. Rec'd a letter last evening from Torrey.[56] He seems to be flourishing as well as the others. I will write to you oftener but cannot promise long letters. Also no letter [received] from mother. Think I must drop her a line. Times are getting better, cash circulating plentifully.

Your Brother

D. Townsend

Write often (every mail)

---

53 From this part of the letter to the end, ink is heavy and smeared.

54 This letter was accompanied by a diagram of the building, reproduced in this book.

55 This brief addition was written on the verso of the December 26 letter. It was composed hurriedly, ink dark and smeared.

56 Meacham, 17-18 Torrey had been living and working in Worcester, Mass. for the Washburn Wire Mill. In August 1855, he and his brother Velette, left Worcester, Massachusetts for Iowa. The brothers worked together on building a sawmill. Torrey later purchased prairie land and built his own house in Clay, Iowa, growing oats and wheat in both locations.

Fiddletown Amador Co. Cal Sept 19th 1857

Dear Sister Susan,[57]

I have just rec'd a letter from Aurelia & mother, inclosing some very fine soft light brown hair. I do not know whose head it was clipped from but Aurelia tells me of a fine baby weighing 6 lbs and, as Father says, a perfect facsimile of Susan when she was an infant.[58] Joy to you all I say and may the "little stranger" prove an honor to the race etc. etc. etc. I have no time to spare in writing now. We are well. I send you enclosed a picture of a section of Fiddletown including the Post Office. The street is so narrow that I could not take a very good view. If I could have got nearer a front view, it would have looked better. Hope you will enjoy better health than heretofore. Do write.

Yours Affectionately,

Turn over for the signature [on back of page]

VHS MSC133: 7

---

57 Handwriting scrawled, indicating haste. The daguerreotype mentioned of the Post Office on Main Street is reproduced in this book.

58 The baby was Susan's daughter, Minerva, known as Minnie.

Fiddletown Cal. May 1st/58

Dear Sister [Aurelia]

Yours of Mar 30th has just come to hand. The religious interest you speak of was published in the N.Y. Tribune in detail. Daily prayer meetings have recently been established in Sacramento & San Francisco with similar results though not so extensive.[59]

You do not say whether you received the Cal Magazine.[60] I send it regularly. Is Susan yet confined to her bed? You seem to imply as much. Hope her dear little "Minnie" is now recovered. Mary Emma our little one is now lying in an adjoining room by herself, crowing for her own amusement.[61] What dear little interesting creatures babies are anyhow! It seems to me that no one who is not a parent can fully appreciate how sweet they are. I am becoming more and more attached to California. I think it probable that I shall pass the remainder of my life here though I hope sometime to be favored with an opportunity of visiting you all. People in this vicinity are attending more to gardening & agriculture than heretofore—though gold mining is still the chief employment.

Mary Emma is now in one area while I am trying to use the other writing. She was 5 months old the 27th of last month. How are Brother Herrick's eyes, is he still preaching?

Excuse these few lines. I have to write briefly or not at all.

Your Affectionate Br.

Dennis

How are Orson wife & family getting on?[62] Wrote to parents last mail.

59 *Sacramento Daily Union*, April 10, 1858. General "union" prayer meetings were announced for those of all denominations and held at different locations. "The movement in question is in similar response to meetings which have been held in the East, among all the churches..." May 15, 1858,"We are advised that, although there is an absence of excitement, the religious interest in the community is increasing."

60 *Hutchings' Illustrated* California *Magazine* http://www.yosemite.ca.us/library/hutchings_california_magazine/ was published in San Francisco from 1856-1861. It was a general interest magazine that contained articles that focused on different aspects of California: its mountain scenery, birds, animals, mining, Yosemite, excursions to places of interest, people, events etc.

61 Mary Emma Townsend was born on November 27, 1857.

62 Meacham,5. In 1836, Orson had purchased the family farm in Reading from his father. He endured misfortunes on the farm including family illness.He died August 24, 1865 at age 57, leaving behind his wife and four children.

Montpelier   Mrs. Aurelia Herrick

Fiddletown Ca. Feb 17th 1860

Dear Sister,

Yours has just come to hand and that I may not fail to answer it, I write now, although I have but a moment to spare, as I have the <u>mail</u> to make up for the <u>Atlantic States this evening.</u>

It most always happens that I am more busy at the time when I receive letters from friends east, from the fact that generally it is on the eve of the departure of the <u>mail steamer;</u>[63] again if I don't answer immediately I am apt to neglect it altogether. But enough of this or my introduction will be the substance of my letter—

I am in good health—wife & child have been absent on a visit three weeks. They were well last account.

Working odd spells I have enclosed a few acres of ground, and intend if I have time to take in a good garden spot on the creek ¼ mile from town and raise my own vegetables—We are living easy though not getting rich very fast. Sent for a melodeon to Providence R.I. which arrived six weeks ago.[64] I am trying to learn to play at odd moments, have a work on Thorough Base and a stack of music books of different kinds—I have taught several singing schools[65] since arriving here—have one in full blast now—I take pictures as I have calls; though this branch is not rushing. I make it pay whenever I have applicants. Photography is really a science and very interesting. I have often thought that it would suit Br. Herrick's turn of mind, he used to be so fond of chemical experiments, but I suppose that it would not be favorable to his eyes, or rather, he eyes would not be favorable to the art.

The longer I stay in California the better I like. It is true we are still lacking some of the blessings belonging to older States, in point of religious and <u>intellectual advantages</u> and refined society, though a rapid improvement is

63 By the 17th of the month, Dennis needed to process outgoing mail for the steamship departure on the 20th, leaving little time to respond to recently arrived personal letters.

64 Was this a second melodeon or a replacement for the one purchased in 1854 for Lizzy, noted in the April 18, 1856 letter to his parents? It seems unlikely that their home had two of these upright instruments.

65 Singing schools were very popular in communities during the 19th century. In New England, singing schools grew quickly in connection with congregational singing in Protestant churches.

going on in these particulars—I will continue sending the Cal Magazine if you like it. I send it regularly to Eliza. What have I written? I must close any how—write often as you promise, and believe me, it should not be through any <u>intended</u> neglect if I am remiss in this respect—Every alternate Sabbath we have preaching by a circuit Methodist preacher—We have good singing—I lead the choir—A young married man is teaching the school here—If I had not gone into the picture business I could have retained the school and had considerable more prosperity this day.[66] Tell me confidentially some particulars of Br Fay.[67] Mother made some general remarks but nothing definite—I hope for the best in Susan's behalf.

Affectionately,

Dennis Townsend

VHS MSC133: 7

---

66 This part of the letter is scrawled with ink blots. The handwriting is messy, indicating haste.

67 Meacham, 15 and 18. Susan had married Ezra Fay on May 24, 1855 but divorced him in 1858. He "proved to be something of a tyrant." Susan returned with her daughter Minnie to the family home in Felchville. Mr. Fay also lived close by.

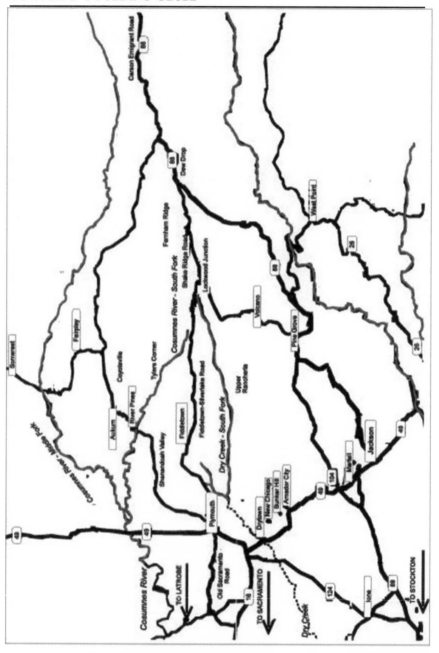

Figure 10. Roads leading to and from Fiddletown follow historic routes.

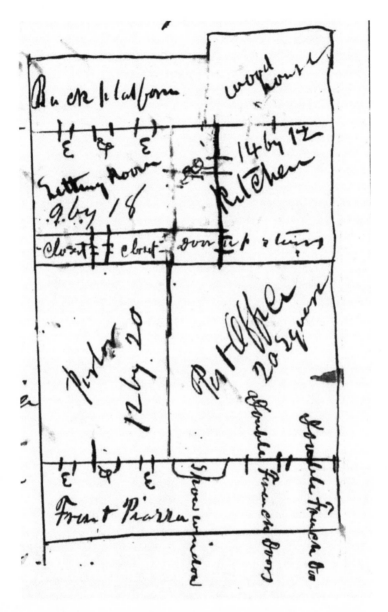

Figure 11. Diagram of Townsend quarters from Letter to Sister, December 24, 1856: *Vermont Historical Society*

Figure 12. Fiddletown East Main Street, 1857 by Dennis Townsend: *Amador County Archives.*

Figure 13. Lynching of Rafael Escobar after Rancheria Massacre, 1855: *Amador County Archives*

Figure 14. Hutchings' The Mammoth Trees, 1854: *Courtesy of the California History Room, California State Library, Sacramento, California*

81

CHAPTER 4

Schoolteacher in a Tumultuous Decade

The remainder of the 1860s decade brought about major changes for the California Townsends. After pursuing several vocations, Dennis refocused his energies on the profession of teaching, where his abilities led to a responsible position as Amador County Superintendent of Schools. On August 23, 1861, Dennis and Lizzy welcomed a new family member, their son also named Dennis Townsend. On the national scene the American Civil War, which erupted in April 1861, split the Union and the Townsend family, placing some members on opposite sides of the conflict.

Teacher

Fiddletown in 1860 had a population of 1119 of which at least one-third consisted of immigrants from China. Gold mining continued to be a major endeavor, but not on the scale of the early Gold Rush or the large industrial deep-shaft quartz mines that arose along the towns to the southwest, strung from Plymouth to Jackson. With farms sprinkled throughout Fiddletown and its outskirts, farming and ranching became an alternative pursuit to mining. Agriculture expanded in the 1860s as new homesteads brought more land under cultivation, accelerated by the passage of the 1862 Homestead Act.[1]

Dennis' desire to gain financial security always bedeviled him. Despite his efforts, prosperity seemed to be elusive. In a newsy letter to Aurelia written on February 28, 1862, he related that he had taught school for six months in 1861 and would continue to teach that year. In addition, he instructed in several singing schools. Calculating living expenses at about $100 a month, Dennis' teaching jobs covered that and "a little more." Did he still have the newspaper and stationery store? He didn't reveal his other activities nor did he provide details about the school where he taught or its students.

In 1862 a new one-room schoolhouse replaced Fiddletown's 1855 school. It was built on a steep hill, across from the Fiddletown burial

1 This legislation, passed during the Civil War, granted 160 acres of public land to those citizens and prospective citizens who could improve it in five years. It promoted settling the country in areas that had been Indians' land.

grounds on the street known then as Church Street, now called American Flat. The new building could accommodate additional students in its spacious front room. Classes were large and crowded—102 students enrolled in 1861 and 117 students in 1862.[2] With students ranging in age from preschoolers through the early teens, it took a firm hand for a teacher to maintain order in the classroom. Comforts and supplies were at a minimum—students of different ages and sizes were seated on hard benches or small desks; a wood burning stove provided warmth on cold winter days. A teacher or student helper had to start a fire every morning, continuing to stoke it with wood during class.[3] Water for the children to drink needed to be carried uphill in buckets by designated students. There were no standardized readers or learning aids, and toilets were in outhouses—two-seaters for the girls and one for the boys.

The challenges of teaching did not discourage Dennis. He had made the choice to dedicate himself to the profession. In mid-1861, he resigned as Postmaster of Fiddletown. He was replaced by Henry Barnhisel, who boarded with the Townsends and worked in the news and stationery shop. Barnhisel, identified as a stationer in the 1860 Census, did not stay long as Postmaster.[4]

Family and Civil War

The decade of 1860 brought sorrow to the Townsend siblings—illness to Aurelia and divided loyalties among the siblings. Aurelia in 1860 had disclosed to Susan that she had a cancerous breast tumor; her siblings were most sympathetic to her suffering. Dennis expressed compassion for her situation coupled with a fatalistic faith in God.

California had entered the Union in 1850 as a slave-free state, upsetting the balance of slave-free and slave states. The status of any newly accepted state became a critical point of contention between pro-slavery

2 California State Land Office Records, R 388 [Series 12] [Box41/1] *School Fund Apportionment Reports. Annual Census returns* 1861-1869 (California State Archives, Office of the Secretary of State, Sacramento, CA.) Only white children were counted in the Census. Black, Indian, Chinese children, if attending schools, were not counted.

3 Zimmerman, Jonathan, *Small Wonder: The Little Red Schoolhouse in History and Memory*, (New Haven, Yale University Press, 2009) and Zorbas, Elaine, *Fiddletown Schoolhouse Memories*, Fiddletown Preservation Society, 2015.

4 https://about.usps.com/who/profile/history/postmaster-finder/postmasters-by-city. htmn. Barnhisel was Postmaster for less than two years: from 6/19/1861 until 4/15/1863 when Townsend again resumed the position. See Zorbas, *Fiddletown, 54* for an iconic daguerreotype of Barnhisel as a miner. There is no attribution to the photographer.

factions and abolitionists throughout the 1850s. Despite California's status as a slave-free state, slaves were brought to the state by Southerners who settled there.[5] Dennis had revealed broad-mindedness towards people from various backgrounds and religions in his letter of August 31, 1855.[6] When the Know Nothing Party—anti-immigrant, anti-Catholic, anti-Chinese—rose to power in 1855, he clearly declared his distaste for that position. As a Californian, he continued to encounter people of different races and nationalities.

In the 1860 election Dennis voted for Stephen A. Douglas, a Vermonter by birth and a three term Senator from Illinois. Douglas, an advocate of popular sovereignty in the new U.S. territories, supported a method that would allow people living in those regions to vote on whether to accept or exclude slavery. Potentially, popular sovereignty could lead to the spread of slavery in newly settled territories encompassing a large swathe of the southwest and northwest.[7] Douglas, a Democrat, faced Abraham Lincoln, who represented the anti-slavery Republican Party, and John C. Breckinridge, nominated by secessionist Southern Democrats. Only white men had the privilege of voting.

Dennis affirmed in his November 23, 1860 letter that he would be amenable to a Republican administration, despite having voted for Douglas. After Abraham Lincoln won the election of 1860, the nation catapulted towards civil war. Prior to Lincoln's inauguration, seven Southern states seceded: Georgia, Alabama, Mississippi, Texas, South Carolina, and Florida. There were various attempts for a peaceful settlement, but by April 12, 1861, the conflict had begun.[8]

Both of Dennis' brothers, William and Alfred spent years living in the South and held similar positions regarding slavery. William in 1847 farmed in Louisiana, claiming that he had two families—one his wife, children and an overseer, and the other a Black family of slaves, consisting of three men, two women and four children. William's attitude towards his slaves was paternalistic. He declared, "Mine fare like others who have

5 The 1850 Fugitive Slave Act although not always enforced in California and some northern states, required escaped slaves to be returned to their enslavers. It was finally officially repealed in August, 1864.

6 He did not refer to race and the cruelty of slavery until much later. Dennis was not an Abolitionist nor politically active.

7 In 1860, territories were large areas not yet defined by state lines identified as New Mexico, Utah, Nebraska, Washington territories, as well as Indian Territory above Texas.

8 See Nevins, Alan, *War for the Union: Vol. 1, The Improvised War, 1861-1862*, New York, Konesky & Konesky, 1971. 6-36.

good masters," averring that they have plentiful food to eat and a day off Saturday afternoons to work in their gardens and tend to their chickens.[9] As William's farm prospered, he left its management to a hired overseer while he spent time establishing and staffing four singing schools

Alfred, living in Texas from 1851 to 1852, received several Black slaves from a slave trader as payment for $1,600 unpaid debt. They included two women, one child and a boy of 17, "worth $2,000." Alfred hired out one of the women for work, bringing him an income of $200 for an unspecified time. In 1853, he relocated to Louisiana, the same state where his brother William resided. Alfred maintained that slaves of the South were "better off and happier than the poor Negroes of the North... the slaves who have kind masters would not leave them under any circumstances." He hoped that slavery could be "done away with," but by a natural and orderly settlement of the question, not by abolitionists, declaring in a letter that "Their course is not bettering the conditions of slaves." [10]

William later wrote from Clinton, Louisiana that the farm was left to his wife's daughter by her deceased father. At this time, William had a large family with nine children. Identifying himself as a Methodist, William reverted to his passion of preaching. Dennis noted in his letter of August 31, 1855 that William was preaching to Blacks, wryly commenting, "I suppose he is trying to tread the path of duty." William stanchly defended the South before and after the outbreak of the Civil War. He wrote in May 1861, "...the South can never be brought into subjugation by those Black Republicans. We are conscientious in our position. If God be for us, who can be against us."

In a moving and eloquent letter written on September 9, 1861 to Aurelia, Dennis expressed his strong support for maintaining the Union, even though the costs would be heavy. Upon receiving a letter from William, who made his pro-slavery opinion known, Dennis suggested to his sister Aurelia that they moderate what they wrote to their southern brothers. Expressing any anti-slavery views could place their brothers in jeopardy with their fellow southerners. By avoiding any written discussion about the issue of slavery and the secession of the South, they protected their brothers as a way of preserving family harmony. William was no longer corresponding with his sister Isabelle, who had strong anti-

9 Meacham, 12, extrapolating from William's letters, added "He [William] looks upon them as members of the family, provides for them and corrects them as a parent would. He believes they all love him."

10 Meacham, 13, 15 quotes and summaries extracted from letters of William and Alfred.

slavery sentiments; Dennis feeling especially close to William and Alfred did not want to endanger that relationship.

By the mid-1850s several of the younger Townsend brothers and sisters departed from New England to settle in Iowa— Francis Torrey (known as Torrey), Velette, Isabelle, Marquis and lastly Eliza, the only unmarried sister.[11] They all supported the Union cause. But the war was wrenching, separating them from their spouses and children. Isabelle and her husband, Henry Waterman, lived in Polk City, Iowa with their five children. In 1862, Henry joined Company B, 23rd Regiment of Iowa volunteers, later serving in a hospital. When he left home for the army, Isabelle wrote an emotional letter to Aurelia:[12]

> I suppose E. [Eliza] wrote you that my dear husband has gone to war. I will not attempt to describe my feelings at the time he enlisted & for weeks since. No one can realize anything about [it] till they have the experience. How many thousands of women are left in the same condition & perhaps worse than I am. Oh! when will this *dreadfull* war cease! how much suffering it has already caused & how much it is to cause in [the] future we know not.

That same year, Marquis, the youngest of the family, enlisted in the Union Army, leaving behind in Iowa his wife and young daughter. He fought in the Vicksburg siege and sustained injuries, afterwards discharged for disability. He regretted "not being able to stay to help crush this accursed rebellion from our land."[13] Torrey was drafted as a member of the 13th Iowa Infantry in October 1864; his absence deeply affected his wife and three children. In his autobiography Torrey related his movements during the war, describing the rout of General Hood's Confederate Army near Nashville, Tennessee and his subsequent hospitalization for illness. He reported that General Hood lost about 15,000 men, including prisoners, his army defeated in a fierce battle.[14] Velette also had relocated to Iowa, joined in 1857 by Eliza who took care of his ailing wife and young child. After his wife's death, he moved back to Worcester, Massachusetts and Eliza followed afterwards in 1864. The rest of the family—Elmer, Buren,

---

11 Meacham, 17-19

12 Letter from Isabelle Waterman to Aurelia Herrick from Polk City, Iowa, November 24, 1862. VHS MSC133:10. Transcribed by Leslee Mayo.

13 Meacham, 22.

14 Townsend, F.T. *Autobiography,* 37-44. Torrey contracted chronic diarrhea in the army which left him an invalid for the year after the war and permanently affected his health.

Aurelia, Orson, Alstyne, Susan and their parents, William and Hannah Bigelow Townsend—remained in New England.

Mail between North and South was disrupted by the war. In February 1861, two months before the Civil War broke out, the Confederacy established its own Post Office. While the U.S. banned mail exchanges in August 1861 between North and South, it expedited letter delivery between Union soldiers in war zones and citizens back home.[15] Some of the siblings living in the North continued to write letters during the war, but there is no known correspondence from Dennis for almost three years —between February 23, 1862 and January, 1865. The Civil War dragged on through the spring and early summer of 1865 when correspondence resumed.

Move to Volcano, Superintendent of Schools

During this hiatus of letter writing, Dennis and his family relocated to Volcano, where he taught in the public school. Dennis updated the entire family in a letter written to his parents, brothers and sisters on January 10, 1865. It was penned shortly after he had recovered from a severe respiratory illness. In the main body of the letter Dennis proclaimed that he and family were in good health, but in an added note to his father he confessed that that he had been acutely ill earlier that winter, intimating that he did not expect to live long if he again suffered a similar lung disorder. This was a reoccurrence of debilitating bouts of illness that affected his lungs

Dennis made the move to Volcano about June 1863, just after serving a short second stint as Postmaster.[16] Lizzy and their two children, Mary Emma and Dennis, Jr. followed six months later after renting out their house in Fiddletown. Lizzy and her sister, Mrs. Margaret Kingsley opened a boarding house in Volcano, hoping to augment the family income. Boarding houses were common in the 19th century and their prevalence during and after the Gold Rush provided women with a good but laborious way to earn a living.[17] The first name of Lizzie's sister Margaret is not given in the letters; her husband, Edward A. Kingsley was prominent in

15 "Mail Service and the Civil War – USPS" pdf.

16 Dennis does not mention resuming his postal duties, but postal records show that he temporarily returned to work at the Post Office on April 15, 1863. The position was filled in next year on February 6, 1864 by Samuel Miller.

17 Levy, *Elephant*, 95-103 and Gamber, Wendy, *The Boardinghouse in Ninetieth-Century America*, (Johns Hopkins, University Press, 2007).

local and county affairs. In 1860, he was appointed township Constable. The next year he was elected county supervisor representing Township 3, which included Volcano.

By 1860 Volcano's population numbered 1,670, beginning a decline from its halcyon days of just a few years before. Mining was still central to its prosperity, but hydraulic mining, a new and destructive method of extracting gold from gravel overtook simpler forms. Large hoses with nozzles known as *monitors* directed high pressure jets of water to wash down masses of potential gold-bearing rocks from hills and mountains, forever changing the landscape and clogging the rivers below.

The town of Volcano had changed by the late 1850s, no longer besieged by new emigrants to California arriving by the Volcano Cut-off. From a raucous mining camp, it evolved into vibrant community with trappings of civilization that included an engaged and creative populace. Its main street featured a few expensive fire-proof stone and brick buildings, replacing some of the flammable wooden structures.[18] The town had a debating society (Lyceum), a subscription library, and an amateur theatre company. The countywide newspaper, the *Volcano Ledger*, published there in 1855, morphed two years later into the long-lived *Amador Ledger*, headquartered in Jackson. Diarist John Doble, residing Volcano when the Townsends arrived, served several terms as elected Justice of the Peace in the late 1850s, as well as providing notary public services. In 1861, astronomy aficionado George Madeira, Jr. built the first amateur observatory in California and on June 30, 1861 he was among the first to site the luminous Great Comet blazing across the clear night sky. He had made the overland journey to Volcano with his family in 1852 and remained in the town for ten years.[19]

When the Townsends moved to Volcano, Dennis taught at Volcano School for $100 per month for terms of five months. This was another large and demanding school with 109 students enrolled in 1863.[20] Yet busy as he must have been, Dennis sought another challenge, assuming more respon-sibilities. That year, he successfully ran for the elected position of Amador

---

18 *Logan's Alley*, Vol.II, 37-47 details the history of several buildings and states that "Volcano's peak of prosperity and promise probably occurred in the fall of 1855."

19 *Logan's Alley*. Vol. III 118-125 covers George Madeira, his family and his observatory.

20 Volcano Schoolhouse, built in 1855, is located on Plug and National Street. It was enlarged into a two-room school about 1880 after Union School rejoined the Volcano District. The smaller one-room version of the schoolhouse building still stands, used as a private residence.

County Superintendent of Common Schools, a job that he held for the next two years at $600 per year. From his letter of January 25, 1865, financial concerns contributed to his motivation for seeking public office. The increase in salary helped to pay for higher expenses in California as the family struggled to emerge from debt. Dennis assumed the new position of school superintendent in March of 1864 while he apparently continued to teach school, performing both jobs for a period. He did not have the time or opportunity to participate in Volcano's social and cultural activities.

Public education was undergoing changes, becoming more systematic and professionalized. Reformers, inspired by Horace Mann and others, urged public support through taxation for common schools, which had been primarily funded by tuition, private donations and land sales. They advocated broadening the curriculum to include knowledge that would allow all students, rich and poor, to better participate in a democracy.[21] As schools started to spread throughout the California and Amador County in the early 1860s, new state legislation provided more standardization and improved public funding. These improvements included state certification of teachers, teacher's institutes for continued training, increasing the annual length of terms, and requiring teachers to take daily attendance as well as give student progress reports. Instead of students providing their own books, standardized textbooks were gradually adopted for teaching geography, history, arithmetic, reading, spelling and grammar. Yet it was not until 1867 that public schooling became tuition free.[22]

One-room schoolhouses, placed within walking distance for students, multiplied in Amador County's many small communities. Amador County contained twenty-four school districts, the smallest containing twenty-seven children (Central House), and the largest with 205 children located in Jackson, the county seat.[23] As Superintendent of Schools in 1864 and 1865, Dennis oversaw these school districts, taking on administrative duties and perhaps making site visits to some schools scattered throughout the county. Dennis presented his *carte de visite,* much like a business card, displaying his portrait. His bearded rather formidable appearance would

21 Neem, *Democracy's Schools,* 87-91, 139-141.

22 Mason, 267-273 and Swett, John, *History of the Public School System in California* (San Francisco, A.L. Bancroft, 1876). Mason covers early changes in public schools in the state and in Amador County. John Swett was elected Superintendent of Schools in 1862 and introduced many reforms.

23 California State Land Office Records R388 [Series 12] *School Fund Apportionment Reports.* The school districts are itemized for each county. The number of districts is based on the August 33, 1863 semi-annual report.

have been emphasized by piercing blue eyes. In those days, people did not smile during the extended time it took to take their photographs.

Dennis achieved the respect from the teachers under his leadership at annual Teachers' Institutes, funded by $150 allocated by the State. These annual meetings, which he organized, were designed to update and train teachers in the best practices. He must have set a fine example for other teachers, because they petitioned the Amador Board of Supervisors on September 10, 1864 to increase the County Superintendent's salary from $600/year (i.e. $50/month) which "is not a sufficient sum to command the necessary ability for the position." Part of the petition reads:

> We the undersigned teachers in this county and assembled together at the Teachers' Institute after due consultation have unanimously concluded that the compensation allowed the County Superintendent by your honorable board is entirely inadequate for the services rendered. They consider that the service has been well performed & has been the means of elevating & improving our common schools in the county; that the labor now devolving upon the Superintendent consequent upon the increased number of children & schools in this county & the requirements of the new school laws have very much increased the necessary labors of the Superintendent. They would also further state that the Supervisors of other counties have generally increased the salaries of their Superintendents.[24]

The petition was signed by seventeen teachers. Despite their overwhelming support for Dennis as Superintendent of Schools, Amador County Supervisors denied the request. The following year, Dennis organized another Teacher's Institute to continue the education of those in the profession.[25]

The Townsends experienced a major setback when a fire broke out in their house on May 2, 1865, related in Dennis' letter of May 28, 1865. Volcano was no stranger to fires, which raged through many foothill towns. Many frame buildings were incinerated in previous fires of 1853 and 1859. The fire of 1865 burnt through two sides of Main Street in the town's oldest section, consuming all the wooden buildings, Chinese stores and many residences, including that of the Townsends. Total losses

---

24 Amador County, "Petition of School Teachers of Amador County for an increase of Salary of County Superintendent, "September 10, 1864. Amador County Archives.
25 Elizabeth and Jesse Mason to Mrs. Jesse Mason, Greensboro, Vermont, August 28, 1867. Amador County Archives. Historian Jesse Mason ran for Amador County Superintendent of Schools in 1867. The salary still remained at $50 per month "for work done mostly at home." He lost the election.

were estimated at $25,000.[26] Dennis, whose family was fortunately visiting Fiddletown at the time, projected his loss at $1,000, including his books and official papers. More work fell upon him as a consequence. His letters do not mention that the Townsends had purchased their house and lot in Volcano, another factor that would have set them back financially.[27]

One result of the fire was family separation. Lizzy and the children returned to live in their Fiddletown house, while Dennis stayed behind in Volcano, boarding with Lizzy's sister, Margaret Kingsley. The distance between the two towns had been reduced in 1855 by a shorter route on a new toll road.[28] Instead of paying for travel by stage, Dennis walked the distance to visit his family, an arduous jaunt of four hours, up and down steep hills.

Conclusion of the Civil War

At the same time that Dennis was teaching and acting as Superintendent of Schools, the Civil War continued to disrupt and destroy lives. Although California entered as a slave free state, not all Californians were pro-Union. Slavery had been outlawed in the state by its constitution, but as mentioned, Southern slave owners had been allowed to bring African American slaves to California and their sentiments remained with the South during the Civil War. One of the two countywide newspapers, the *Amador Dispatch*, sympathized with the South and was known as a "Copperhead" publication.[29] During the Civil War, Dennis' brother-in-law, Edward A. Kingsley served as 2nd Lt. in the Volcano Blues, a pro-Union state militia infantry company, ostensibly organized to counter Confederate sympathizers in Volcano.[30] When Dennis ran a second time

---

26 Mason, 210-211 regarding fires.

27 Amador County, *Judges Certificate Volcano*, April 1871 and *Amador County Map of Volcano, 1870*, July 1937. The D. Townsend house, lot 3, block 9 is shown on Main Street between Consolation and Baptist streets.

28 Zorbas, *Fiddletown*, 39. Dennis estimated a distance of 10 miles between the towns in his letter of June 14, 1866.

29 *Logan's Alley*, Vol. I, 142-143. In Amador County animosity was strong towards Copperheads, Democrats who were anti-War and anti-Lincoln. Because of its views, the *Amador Dispatch* newspaper was forcibly shut down in May 1865 and its editor arrested, a month after Lincoln was assassinated.

30 *Logan's Alley*, Vol. III, 42-64, recounts the saga of the Volcano Blues, who never participated in military action, but managed to acquire a cannon for Volcano, known as "Old Abe."

for the Superintendent of Schools office in the 1865 election, he was defeated by S.G. Briggs, whom he labelled a Copperhead.[31]

Only five days after the April 9, 1865 surrender of Confederate General Lee, President Abraham Lincoln was tragically assassinated. In his letter to Aurelia on May 28, 1865, Dennis expressed relief about the end of the war and the arrest of John Wilkes Booth, assassin of the "great and beloved president." He hoped that the end of slavery would bring about a promising future for the country. His brother Torrey, still in the hospital, "received the sad news of the death of our President, Abraham Lincoln." Upon Torrey's recovery, he travelled from Nashville to Washington, D.C. to link up with his regiment as part of General Sherman's triumphant army. Joining other regiments in Louisville, Kentucky, their brigade camped there until July 22, after General Sherman bid them farewell on July 4.[32]

Now that the war was over, Dennis' brother Alfred resumed writing letters in June 1865 inquiring whether his parents were still alive. He hoped to visit the family home in Vermont. During the war, he had suffered in the South for taking a position as a conservative Union supporter. Although he and William both lived in Louisiana, Alfred only found out a year later that William died on September 9, 1864 at age fifty. He related this sorrowful news to the family in an August 1865 letter.[33]

Without the extra salary for the Superintendent position, Dennis once again relied upon a monthly teacher's salary of $100, the same amount as his estimated cost of living. John Swett, the progressive California Superintendent of Schools, elected in 1862, lamented the low salaries of teachers:

> No occupation is more laborious; none wears out muscle and brain faster. It is only in the vigor of early manhood that a man can follow his profession. Shall he, then, be paid no more than the mechanic, or the day labor who shovels sand in the streets? The skillful teacher ought to be as the brain labor of the lawyer, the physician, the clergyman, the editor.... He should be paid enough to support a family.[34]

31 Mason, 272. Rev. S. G. Briggs served as Superintendent of Schools from 1866-1875. His brother R.G. Briggs was prominent in the county as the elected Amador County District Attorney.

32 Townsend, F.T. *Autobiography*, 40-43. Torrey farmed in Iowa before and after the war,

33 Meacham, 23-24 and Vermont Historical Society *William Townsend family Letters 1827-1899*, MSC 133 (Barre, Vermont, 2004, rev. 2020) Finding aid, 3. Alfred moved back to Texas in 1868, but died suddenly on March 10, 1871.

34 Swett, 50. See also Kathleen Weiler, *Country Schoolwomen: Teaching in Rural*

Dennis continued to teach at Volcano School after the losing the election, enrolling as many as 145 students. In two letters written in June, 1866, he articulated his passion and love for teaching. He strove to continually learn and improve, considering Volcano School to be the finest school in the county. Committed to teaching despite its paltry remuneration, Dennis exemplified the best of his chosen profession.

For news of the family, Dennis depended on his sisters, Susan, Eliza, and Aurelia. After her divorce in 1858, Susan lived with her daughter Minnie in the family home in Felchville, a village within the sphere of Reading, Vermont. Eliza returned to this home after Velette remarried. The sisters' hopes for financial benefits from an estate in England were not encouraged by Dennis and apparently never materialized.

Dennis longed for family members to send their portraits, but apart from taking a picture of his five year-old son, it seems that Dennis had little time to photograph his wife and daughter. Lizzy, now living in Fiddletown with two young children and having many household duties, was also short of time to write to her own family as well as to her in-laws. Perhaps to assuage his distant family, Dennis wrote that he and Lizzy managed to live comfortably, even if mostly apart.

There are important omissions in Dennis' correspondence about the deaths that occurred in the family, perhaps attributable to infrequent or missing letters and a delay in relaying the news. His older brother Orson died on April 9, 1865. Yet Aurelia wrote to Dennis that same month on April 14, 1865 without mentioning the death; from Dennis' May 28th response, there is no indication that he ever received that sad news. Orson had tended the family farm in Reading, purchased from his father around 1836. The farm never thrived and he left behind a wife and four children.[35] The patriarch of the family, William Townsend died several months later on December 19, 1865, but no surviving letters of Dennis refer to the death of his esteemed father. Six months later in his June 9, 1866 letter, Dennis disclosed to his step-mother [Hannah G. Bigelow] his love and admiration for her, with no reference to his deceased father or her situation as a widow.

On August, 10, 1867 Dennis wrote a hurried letter to his sister Susan from Fiddletown, referring to news about family members. He was on summer break in Fiddletown but in three weeks, he would resume teach-

California, 1850-1950 (Stanford, CA, Stanford University Press, 1998), 36-39. In 1860 California schools, 536 teachers were men, and 281 teachers were women. Swett encouraged women to enter teaching, noting their superior emotional abilities.
35 Meacham, 4.

ing in Volcano. Dennis had reached fifty years old and he now appeared tired and discouraged by the heavy load of teaching, which occupied all of his time.

The following year, he departed on his own for Boston and the family home in Vermont. His many years teaching school had given him an idea for a tool to aid classroom instruction, an invention yet to be fully conceptualized and fabricated. Dennis planned on bringing the planet Earth into the classroom.

Letters: 1860 - 1867

Fiddletown Amador Co Cal Nov 23 1860

Dear Sister [Aurelia]

I heard of your misfortunes by Susan's letter, but do not recollect of your alluding to them in any letter before the one rec'd a few days since. I deeply sympathize with you and hope all will work to your advantage in the end.

I have been very busy of late but not very prosperous. Times have been rather stringent and money scarce; however we get along comfortably, enjoy health and have no great reason to complain in any point of view. I do really hope the tumor you speak of may prove to be nothing serious.[1] Don't borrow any trouble about it but I hope that it may not prove to be anything worse than has befallen others and caused no alarm or real injury. From your account I judge that Mr. Herrick and yourself will be more pleasantly situated in your new situation than heretofore. In any event I think it our duty to "make the best we can of life nor render it a curse" as Father used to sing so often.

Since the day of the presidential election our little village has been very quiet. All seem to be calmly waiting to hear of the result though we rec'd news sufficient to establish 's election beyond a doubt. I voted for Douglas & Johnson. I never take an active part in politics, and think I can live under a Republican administration very well.

The weather is delightful, the winter rains not having set in yet. You can have no idea of the clearness of the atmosphere here. I heard a gentleman remark who had returned to his native state N.Y. that during his stay, no day during the summer however bright seemed to be clear, so great was the contrast between the skies of & N.Y.

I write in much haste. In fact I always do. Excuse, I will send the Cal Mg. [California Magazine] as you desire with pleasure. We do not regard it as occupying a high rank as a literary periodical but the articles and illustrations being chiefly Californian, it is generally interesting to subscribers east. I am glad to learn of the prosperity of Buren[2]. I think the "second crop" as father

---

1 Meacham, 19 refers to a letter written to Aurelia that same month by their brother Elmer who expressed hope that an operation would cure her. Aurelia did have surgery for breast cancer. It was arrested for a number of years, but later resurfaced.

2 Meacham, 21. Buren (Van Buren), married in 1858 and remained in New England. He lived in Worcester, Mass., working as a teamster (driving a team of horses) for the Washburn Wire Mill, which fabricated wire for ladies' apparel, hair pins, hooks & eyes.

used to call them are all well calculated to prosper. I have not rec'd a letter from any relation in many months, when your last reached me dated Oct 17th. Our little daughter three years old on the 27th of this month is a great joy and comfort to us.

Your Br

Dennis Townsend

VHS MSC133: 7

(Rec'd Oct 7th '61)

Fiddletown Amador Co Cal Sept 9th 1861

Dear Sister Aurelia

It is with pain that I am informed of your continued suffering. If I could do anything to relieve you, I would joyfully to it; but I have nothing but my sympathy to offer you which though it may be some slight consolation, cannot alleviate a single pang.

It is doubtless our duty under all circumstances to be as cheerful as possible, and resigned to whatever affliction we may be called to pass through under Providence, but while the "Spirit is willing the flesh is weak," and on this ground charity should be extended to the repining. "Hope keeps the heart whole." Let us hope for the best, and rest in unwavering confidence that all will be well finally. We live in troublous times. Our government, the most beneficent ever devised by man is having an ordeal truly terrific. The worst feature of which is that it literally involves in deadly strife brother with brother, father with son. I am with those who say the government must be maintained cost what it may of blood and treasure. I have no fears for the result of the struggle which I doubt not will command the gratitude of unborn millions. If they were alive what would now be the voice of Washington, Adams, Webster, Jackson & Clay? And what is the voice of every true patriot unbiased by prejudice or personal interest? William and Alfred are peculiarly situated [living in the South] and no person who has always lived in a free state can appreciate the influences that are brought to bear on them. I am not surprised that William expresses himself as he does. It is not best to write him any letters denouncing his course as it might involve him in difficulty instead of doing any good. Situated as our brothers are it would be bad policy for us by our letters to create a suspicion among their southern friends that they are opposed to the southern movement.

A few days since I rec'd letters from Mother Susan & Eliza. I always get a great deal of news by Mothers letters. Susan wrote a long and very interesting letter, though there was a vein of sadness running through the whole, in consequence of the war and its effect on different members of our family—but more particularly on account of your afflictions. Her happiness seems more bound up in yours than in that of any other living being—I hope for the best that you may regain your health, that our lives may long be spared and [that] we may be a comfort to each other in the decline of life. It appears that both father & mother are quite feeble—Dennis Townsend Jr. is two weeks & three days old.[3] They say he resembles me. The nose, blue eyes and prominent upper lip it would be folly for me to deny—Wife is comfortable, up and about the house.

Hope to hear from you often.

Your Aftn [Affectionate] Br [Brother]

Dennis Townsend

---

3 Dennis Townsend, Jr. was born August 23, 1861.

Fiddletown Amador Co Cal Feb 23rd 1862[4]

Dear Sister Aurelia,

Yours of Jan 15th has come to hand. I rejoice to learn that you are so comfortable. Afflictions seem to be unequally divided in the human family though every one [of us] must have a share and outward appearances do not always indicate where the heaviest strokes fall or where the heaviest burdens are borne. If we are fully satisfied that there is a just God whose providence extends to the minutest affairs of life—and I do not doubt it—we should rejoice in our resignation to whatever trials we may be called on to endure, knowing that in the end all will be for the best. I rec'd a letter from parents and Susan some time ago, which I have not yet answered. Father wrote a long letter for him, which I intend carefully to treasure. Mother's letters are interesting as ever. Susan occupied considerable space in discussing the war. I think that if I should get another letter from her soon, I think it would be in a more cheerful strain on that subject. The Union successes in N.C., Ky, Tenn, & Mo. are truly cheering to every patriotic heart.[5] By telegraph we get news of all important events as soon as you do—yes—in less than no time if we note it by hour of the day.[6] The other day a dispatch came from Chicago dated there about 11 o'clock and reached Sacramento about 9 o'clock almost two hours less than no time in crossing the Plains. It took me 168 days to perform that feat with an ox team.

Eliza seems to be very fond of her new employment of teaching Social Music and seems to be considerably elated in her new sphere—I would like very much to have her here. I have taught several Singing Schools here, and have one under way now. The floods in Cal. have surpassed anything ever known here to white men. The whole state has suffered severely and Sacramento our Capital is nearly ruined.[7] The Legislature adjourned to where

---

4 Although the letter is dated February 1862, some events mentioned occurred in the previous year.

5 Kearnes, Doris Goodwin, *Team of Rivals: The Political Genius of Abraham Lincoln*, New York, Simon & Schuster, 2005, 407-418. In February, 1862, Fort Henry and Fort Donelson in Tennessee were captured by the Union Army, its first successful victory in the war. More than 1,000 troops on both sides were killed.

6 Samuel Morse's telegraph was first demonstrated in 1843 between Washington, D.C. and Baltimore. Western Union became dominant among several competing companies, and by 1861 completed the first transcontinental telegraph line that ultimately connected San Francisco to the East Coast. The telegraph revolutionized the transmission of communication and news.

7 Ingram, B. Lynn, "California Megaflood Lessons from a Forgotten Catastrophe," *Scientific American*, January 1, 2013. The floods between December 1861 and January

they are now holding a session. I have just closed a quarter of my school. I taught about half of last year and shall probably teach about six months of this year. I am making a living and perhaps a little more—The fact is it costs me about $100 per month to live—I am no longer PM [Postmaster]. I resigned in favor of a young man by the name of H. Barnhisel[8] who has the office.[9] It is still kept in my house—

Your affectionate

Dennis Townsend

1862 were catastrophic to the entire state—north, south and in the Central Valley. In early January, 1862, Sacramento city, built on the confluence of two rivers (Sacramento and American Rivers) was submerged under 10 feet of water and remained underwater for months. The Central Valley became in inland sea; one third of the State's property was destroyed.

8 Henry Barnhisel assumed Postmaster duties on July 19, 1861 and apparently continued to live in the Townsend's living quarters combined with the post office.

9 The handwriting, neat at the beginning of the letter, becomes scrawled as the letter progresses.

Volcano Amador Co Cal[10] Jan 10th 1865

Dear Parents
Brothers & Sisters[11]

I have just recd mother's letter, forwarded from Fiddletown. I changed my place of residence about 18 months ago to Volcano and moved my family nearly a year ago. Since I last wrote we have enjoyed a share of health ordinarily allotted to humanity though we have all been quite severely affected at times—We are now all enjoying health. I have been teaching in Volcano 14 months at $100 per month and commence another term of 5 months, next Monday, at the same price. I entered upon the duties of Co. Supt. of Common Schools in at a salary of $600 per annum last March. I was elected for two years. I am renting my property at Fiddletown for the present at $26 per month. Expenses are pretty heavy and I am not entirely clear of debt though I can now see my way through. Wife and children send their love. Mary Emma was 7 years old Nov. 27 and Dennis 3 years August 23rd. Have not recd [received] a word from Alfred or Wm. since the rebellion broke out. If you have heard from them please let me know. My wife & Mrs. Kingsley,[12] her sister, have opened a boarding house recently. I think they will do well if they pay half of the expenses of the two families.

My office requires more writing than I anticipated. I sometimes send off 2 dozen letters at a time.

Hope to get letters from you all soon. Marquis write me your experiences in the army[13]—Hope the war will soon end with our country on the high road to prosperity. The curse of slavery being wiped out, we have sure grounds to hope for national greatness in the future—I write in haste—Excuse the disjointed sentences of this letter—I send enclosed the proceedings of our County Teachers Institute—I would like to get letters from each one of you.

---

10 Scrawled above "Direct to Volcano Amador Co Cal – Volcano is 10 miles from Fiddletown"

11 This is Dennis' first letter after almost a 3 year hiatus. It was directed to the family living in New England.

12 The 1860 Census gives the incorrect name of Mary, instead of Margaret as the wife of Edward A. Kingsley. Illinois records for Lizzy's family, show sister Mary A. Ray was married to Thomas Williams and remained in Carrollton, Illinois.

13 The youngest brother, Marquis, fought in the Vicksburg siege and was badly wounded. Dennis must have received letters from a sibling who told him of Marquis' participation in the war.

Affectionately,

Dennis Townsend

Father,[14]

I am sorry to learn that you are suffering as you are. There was a time the 1st of the present winter when I had little hope of anything like health again[15]—I had taken a very severe cold that settled on my lungs. A portion of the matter that I expectorated sunk in water like a shot—My cough has entirely left me now and I feel quite well, but I am satisfied. If I do not take particular care of my lungs, I cannot hope for long life.

VHS MSC133: 7

---

14 This note to father was added to the same letter; handwriting scrawled. In contrast to the main letter, it reveals how ill Dennis had been, also expressing empathy for his father's illness. William Townsend died later that year on December 19, 1865.
15 The weather was harsher in Volcano than in Fiddletown with colder winters that often included snow and heavy rain.

Volcano, Amador Co. May 28th 1865

Dear Sister Aurelia[16]

Yours of Apr 14th is before me. I have just returned from visiting schools and find your letter waiting for me.

More misfortunes—On the night of the 2nd of this month at one o'clock I was aroused by the cry of <u>fire</u>! In a few minutes our house was a mass of flames. I was able to do but little more than to escape with my life. The fire broke out on the street opposite to us.[17] My loss is $1000, more or less. My family had gone to Fiddletown for that day. They will remain there for a while.

I write you these few words thinking that a short letter will be more acceptable to you than none.

I open school again tomorrow. The loss of my books and official papers gives me considerable extra work. Glad to learn that you are comfortably situated. If you hear from Wm or Alfred tell me. I must write a line to Felchville if it is no more than to acknowledge the receipt of Susan & Eliza's letters. I would be glad to receive a letter from Br Herrick if he has time to write.

The storm of rebellion is nearly over, its mutterings only heard over the fields of Texas.[18] J. Davis the arch traitor and assassin of our great & beloved president has been captured and never have the friends of freedom had so great reason to rejoice at the glorious prospects of our republic. Only let the people be wise in the selection of their rulers and all will be well.

Write when you have an opportunity don't wait for me.

Yours affte Br—

Dennis Townsend

16 The copy of this letter is very faint. Dennis' handwriting is scrawled, indicating great hurry. A note is written on the bottom of the letter in a different handwriting, "Answered February '66, Aurelia."

17 Townsend house, lot 3, block 9, was located on Main Street, just a few lots northwest of Consolation, the town's main intersection. The fire started across the street from their house, north of Hanford's store, lot 17, block 1.

18 Texas finally yielded to the Union on June 2, 1865, two months after the war was officially over. Slaves there were not emancipated until June 19, long after the Emancipation Proclamation declaration on January 1, 1863. It is now celebrated as Juneteenth.

Fiddletown, Amador Co., Cal June 9th, 1866

Dear Mother and sisters

Your letters came to hand on the 7th just. We were very glad to receive them and much interested by their contents.

Tuesday the 5th I closed my school for a vacation; shall probably open again in about a month. During the term just closed I enrolled 145 names of pupils. Two school districts supported a Union School[19] and I had an Assistant—I have the credit of teaching the best school in the county. I prefer teaching to any employment in which I can engage and I am conscious of continuing to improve as a teacher by experience, though some may imagine that a man must be past improvement at the age of 49... My wife keeps house here in Fiddletown, while I board with her sister who keeps a boarding house in Volcano. I have a little property and we live comfortably, though it would be much pleasanter if I could be with my family all of the time. Volcano & Fiddletown are about four hours walk from each other.

Mother,[20] I send you a picture of Dennis Townsend, our son who will be five years old the 23rd of next August. Our daughter Mary Emma will be nine years old next November.

I will send pictures of my wife and daughter and perhaps of myself soon. I have none at present.

Nothing could please me better than to visit you, but I am not in circumstances to say whether I shall ever be able to do it.

Susan, I have not received the photographs [you sent] of Minnie Mary and Carrie. Who are Mary & Carrie?[21] I suppose they are Orson's children.

Eliza I have never rec'd any hint that an effort is making to get the Livermore estate[22] except what you have said in your last letter. My hopes

---

19 Mason, 271-272. The Volcano School district split in two in 1861, forming separate districts with a Union School and Volcano School. Around 1880, the two districts merged.

20 This refers to Dennis' much beloved step-mother, Hannah G. Bigelow.

21 Townsend, F.T. *Autobiography,* 17, Susan's daughter Minnie was born 1857; 23, Velette's daughter Mary was born in 1857; 21, Isabelle's daughter Carrie was born in 1862; Marquis also had a daughter named Carrie, also born 1862.

22 The Townsend family's ancestors were from Norfolk, England, a long line of succession. There was hope of an inheritance from a Livermore Estate, but based on family information, it never materialized. According to Liane Fenimore, the Townsend Society genealogist and journal editor, the Livermores were not connected to the Townsends and a supposed marriage in the 17th century between the two families was never substantiated.

are <u>very faintest</u> of a fortune from that source. Please explain definitely if you know what has been done about it—I have witnessed none of the spiritual manifestation that you speak of, though I have read some upon the subject. I have never seen anything on which to found a belief, much less a faith in spiritualism,[23] though I am not disposed to scoff at any doctrine simply because it is opposed to preconceived notions, or because I cannot comprehend it. The idea of being able to converse with our departed friends is certainly a very pleasing one—Mother, I perused your letter with great pleasure. Age seems not to have impaired the vigor of your intellect or the steadiness of your hand—You are very dear to me. I recall the time when you were introduced to me as one who would fill the place of my mother. Recollecting this so distinctly, strange it is that I have not retained the slightest remembrance of my own mother. After the death of Adin being the youngest,[24] and of very tender age when [I was] committed to your care, I have thought if there is any distinction, that I have stood next to your own children in your affections. It grieves me that I have never been able to requite your uniform kindness in a more substantial manner—

Affectionately, *Dennis Townsend*

My wife sends her love and wishes you not to consider her neglect of writing as an evidence of want of regard, for she is so situated that she does not write to her own mother, brother, and sisters so often as the dictates of affection would seem to require.[25]

Susan, can you not send duplicates of the pictures you spoke of.[26]

VHS MSC133: 7

---

23 Braude, Ann, *Radical Spirits: Spiritualism and Women's Rights in Nineteenth Century America*, 2nd edition (Bloomington, IN, Indiana University Press, 1989, 2001). Spiritualism was a widespread religious movement in the 19th century that aimed at proving the immortality of the soul. Intermediaries, many of whom were women in new roles of religious leadership, attempted to communicate with the souls of the dead through séances and trances.

24 Adin was two years younger than Dennis and the last child of his birth mother, Susannah Smith. She died on April 9, 1820 when Adin was almost a year old. Cared for by his step-mother, Adin died at age four in June, 1823.

25 This note was written sideways at the top of the letter in the space before the greeting line.

26 This afterthought was written sideways on right margin of the first page, making it difficult to read the letter.

Volcano Amador Co. Ca. June 14th, 1866

Dear Sister Aurelia,

I have neglected answering your last letter thinking that I should have some photographs to send you in a short time, but I have concluded to delay no longer and will send the pictures when I get them. As your letter is not before me, if it contained any special inquiries I cannot answer them.

I have just closed my school for a vacation, which will probably continue a month or more. I prefer teaching to any other business in which I can engage. The longer I teach the better I like it, and the better qualified I consider myself to conduct a school. My school continues about 10 months in the year[27]—salary $100 per month which is a little more than enough to support my family. Have a little property and am able to live comfortably. Had not the Copperheads[28] out-voted us I should have been retained another term of two years in the office of County Supt. of Schools which would have helped me along some. My family resides in Fiddletown 10 miles distant, as I have a comfortable place for them there, but I have the pleasure of making them frequent visits.

Recd a letter from Mother & Eliza a few days ago. Glad to learn that they are enjoying reasonable health. It has been a long time since I rec'd a word from Susan. They tell me that Alfred contemplates visiting home soon. I wish that I could meet him and you all there. Eliza says another effort is making to get the Livermore Estate in Eng. [England] with a fair prospect of success. I am looking for no windfall in that direction. Tell me if there is anything of it.

I was 49 years of age the 8th of last month. I am pretty well though I think my lungs are slightly affected. During the last year I have enjoyed better health than usual. I have taken a towel bath succeeded by a thorough rubbing, daily, which gives me a freshness of feeling and is a preventative of colds.[29]

Since winter we have had singular weather. The early part of spring was unusually warm, the thermometer going up to nearly 100, but we have since paid for it in cold weather and late frosts, in consequence of which fruit has been injured in some places. Vegetation is flourishing on account of late

---

27 The increased 10 month school year would have covered mid-August to mid-June, with a short two month summer vacation.

28 Copperheads were a faction of Democrats opposed to participating in the Civil War. They opposed the draft and wanted President Lincoln removed from power.

29 Dennis was heath conscious and likely influenced by hydrotherapy.

rains, more than I have ever before witnessed in the state. Crops are excellent everywhere.

August 7th

Shame! Shame that I have not sent this letter before! Next Monday commence schooling again. The hottest weather here this season has raised the thermometer to 109 in the shade, but the air is so pure that the heat has not been very oppressive.[30]

Affectionately Yrs

Dennis Townsend

Let me hear from you.

---

30 This sentence, the signature and the added note are scrawled, the postscript in larger letters with the "you" trailing off.

Fiddletown Amador Co. Cal Aug 10th 1867

Dear Sister Susan,

Yours of July 15th has been recd. Sorry to learn that you have suffered so much but glad that you have been restored to health and that you are now better than you were before your sickness.

Recd a letter from Alfred not long since. He spoke of the marriage of his daughter to a man who had been an officer in the Confederate Navy. Is that an adopted daughter, Albert's child?[31]

Alfred seems to enjoy as good health as usual. It is surprising that he is as well as he is, but I attribute it to the extra care he has taken of himself on account of the frailty of his body.[32]

In three weeks I must return to my old school in Volcano. I shall receive your letters whether directed to Volcano or Fiddletown. In directing you had better continue the practice of naming the county.

Enclosed I send a Family Record[33] as you request—I have never had much expectation of getting anything from the Livermore Estate. It has been lying so long and the matter is now so complicated. Of course, lawyers who are paid for their investigations will hold out encouragement so long as there is any chance to make anything out of it. However I don't pretend to know much about it. I was not prepared to learn that Wm's family were in distressed circumstances. I knew that they were not very prosperous, but did not suppose that they lacked the necessaries of life[34]—I am in a hurry— My school is large and laborious. It occupies my time both in school hours and out. Average daily attendance last month 67 & a fraction. The weather is very warm, thermometer up to about 100 in the shade for many days in succession.[35]

---

31 Townsend, F.T. *Autobiography* 16, and Meacham, 24. Alfred's daughter, Jennie, married Captain Perrin and lived in Louisiana. Alfred's deceased twin, Albert, had two daughters, one who died young, and the other raised by her mother, not adopted.

32 Meacham, 5. Alfred, the surviving twin, had delicate health. When he was 18 years old, he developed pneumonia and ended up with a collapsed lung that plagued him throughout his life.

33 This family record is not among the letters or other papers from the Townsends at Vermont Historical Society.

34 William Townsend Family Letters, 1827-1899 (vermonthistory.org). Alfred wrote in August, 1865 that most of William's family wealth had been invested in slaves. His wife and nine children survived him.

35 Handwriting in this letter is scrawled, mirroring the haste mentioned by Dennis. He was on summer vacation at the time. Fiddletown and Volcano have very hot summers.

Your affectionate brother

Dennis Townsend

Figure 15. Unidentified, likely Lizzy Townsend by Dennis Townsend, 1861: *Amador County Archives*

Figure 16. Fiddletown Schoolhouse circa 1890s: *Fiddletown Preservation Society*

Figure 17. Southwest overview of Fiddletown, 1880s: *Amador County Archives*

Figure 18. Volcano Schoolhouse in the 1950s: *Amador County Archives*

Figure 19. Volcano tintypes circa 1870: *Amador County Archives*

Figure 20. Dennis Townsend calling card: *Dolph Briscoe Center for American History, The University of Texas at Austin*

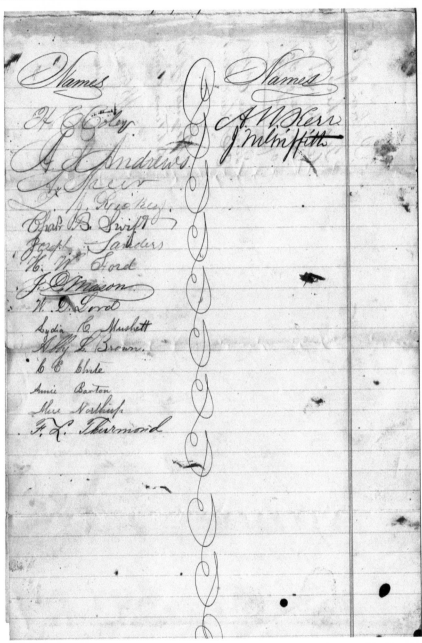

Figure 21. Teachers' Petition signatures for Dennis Townsend: *Amador County Archives*

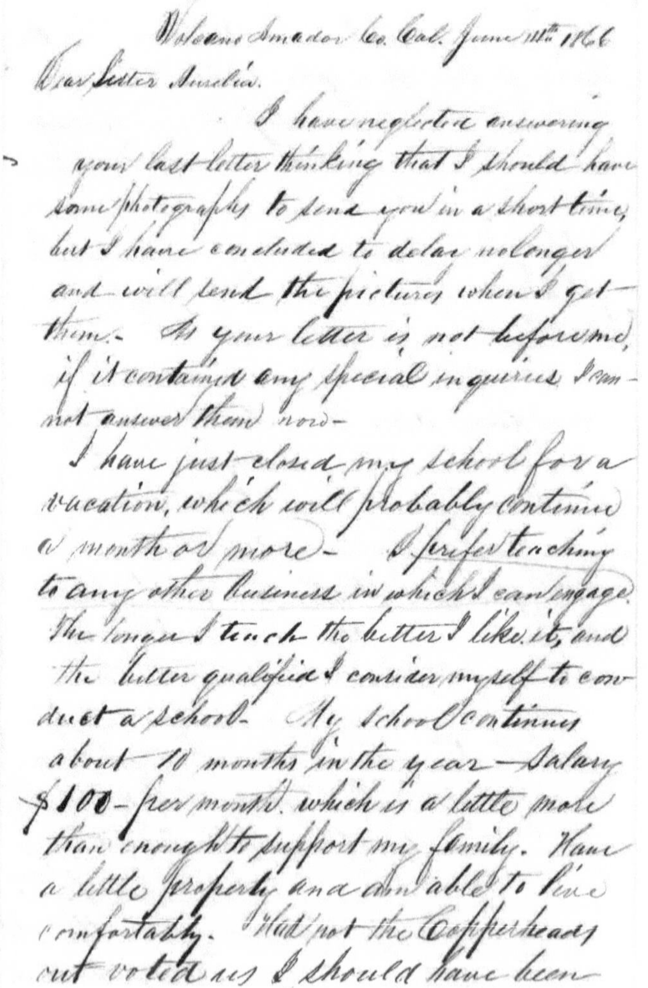

Figure 22. Letter to Aurelia June 14, 1866: *Vermont Historical Society*

CHAPTER 5

Inventing the Globe December 1868-1871

While teaching, Dennis conceived of an invention that percolated in his mind for months and must have become an obsession. As an experienced teacher, he taught geography in school, educating students about concepts of latitude and longitude, the shape of the earth and its trajectory, the location of oceans, the continents and types of land masses. Yet he found that verbal instruction about the earth was not sufficient, nor was a flat two-dimensional map. To truly convey our planet's continents, seas and geographic features, he needed a visual aid, a tool affordable to every classroom. As an alternative to a map, he planned to create a collapsible paper globe that could be expanded into a round orb, intended "to furnish a cheap, convenient, portable article, which can make an excellent substitute for the expensive globe now *occasionally* used in the school room, but to put within the reach of *every family, every child....*"[1]

To bring his idea to fruition, Dennis needed the help of his supportive siblings in New England. Several members of his family were in Vermont or nearby states. Susan, her daughter Minnie, unmarried sister Eliza, and their mother, Hannah Bigelow Townsend, lived together in a frame house in Felchville, a village in the southeast section of Reading that developed in the mid-1830s.[2] Aurelia and her husband moved in 1864 to Wolcott, Vermont after Rev. Horace Herrick gave up his business and resumed his vocation of preaching. Buren and Velette held light manufacturing jobs in Massachusetts. Alstyne worked in a machine shop in Springfield, Vermont.[3]

Dennis especially coveted the approval of his eldest brother, Elmer, hoping to obtain financing from him. As a successful businessman in the boot and shoe trade, Elmer had continued through the years to contribute to the family, offering to pay for Aurelia's board when she was ill,

1 Townsend, Dennis, *Townsend's Folding Globe Lessons: Designed Especially for Family Instruction and the Use of Classes in Schools.* (Burlington, VT, Free Press Print, 1870).

2 Census of 1870. Reading, Vermont had a total population of 1,012, which included Felchville.

3 Meacham, 19, 21 and Townsend, F.T, *Autobiography*, 20. Buren worked at Washburn Wire Mill in Worcester, Mass., as had Torrey and Velette. Alstyne later formed a partnership in the machine shop with his brother-in-law. Their firm, Gilman & Townsend became very successful.

providing items of comfort for their father during his last days, and by sending monthly installments of $50.00 to family members in Felchville. He invested money for Susan and Eliza, sending them interest on bonds.[4]

By autumn 1868 Dennis was on his way back to his New England family to work on his invention, leaving Lizzy and the children behind in Fiddletown. His two letters from December of that year do not reveal how he travelled from California to the East. His choices were limited. The transcontinental railroad was still one year away from completion. The overland journey remained lengthy and arduous. Most likely, Dennis took the Pacific Mail Steamship from San Francisco to Panama City, and then crossed Panama by train to take another steamboat to New York City.[5] As a former postmaster he was familiar with the steamboat's coast-to coast route. In the North and Midwest a network of railroad lines had already been established by 1860, linking most major cities. He might have taken a train or a combination of steamboat and railroad from New York to Boston,[6] where his eldest brother lived and worked.

Dennis stayed with Elmer in Boston for a time. While there, he wrote on October 5 about his oldest brother's reception to his idea. "Elmer is completely converted and enthusiastic in its [folding globe] praise." This businessman brother recognized the potential of making money with the invention and promised aid. Dennis continued, "Everyone gives me credit for entire originality in the invention and all acknowledge its value." On Elmer's advice, Dennis departed for Alstyne's machine shop in Springfield, Vermont to have machinery made and to develop a model of the globe. Dennis took the rest of 1868 and into 1869 to perfect his invention. The thickness of paper had to be just right for folding. He worked on several prototypes for a small, portable 6" globe before he was satisfied.[7]

In December, 1868 Dennis joined the family in Felchville. His letter of December 5, written to Aurelia and Susan [who was visiting her], stat-

---

4 Meacham 22.
5 Coburn, 110. Several ships of the Pacific Mail Steamship Company operated the San Francisco to Panama City route in 1868. After the completion of the transcontinental railroad in 1869, the Pacific mail run from Panama to San Francisco was no longer profitable. Many steamships were sold or transferred to other routes.
6 Steamship Historical Society. The popular Fall River Line route consisted of steamboat travel from Manhattan to Fall River, Massachusetts, connecting there to a railroad leading to Boston.
7 Meacham *Index: Dennis Townsend*, includes quotations extracted from the letters of Dennis, Lizzy and siblings, reproduced here. Dennis apparently wrote about 15 letters from Springfield from October-December 1868, all are missing from the VHS collection except the two reproduced here.

ed Elmer's willingness to make improvements to the house so that they could all comfortably live and work together to manufacture the globe. Dennis expressed gratitude that Elmer, who advised him "to go slow and sure," would not ask him to pay rent during his stay. Another letter sent from Felchville, on December 17, 1868, conveyed Dennis' efforts to improve and fabricate the globe—a spring that would allow it to expand and fold back and a special cutting and folding machine to craft the different elements of his drawing. He reassured Aurelia and Susan that he was feeling well, taking all precautions to stay warm with pampering from his mother and Eliza. But as the letter progressed, it revealed anxiety about fragility of his health, a worry shared by his family.

That year, Dennis was granted an Honorary Degree of Master of Arts from the University of Vermont. The degree was conferred on seven others with Dennis being the only person listed as living in California. The other recipients included two from Chicago and individuals from New York, Vermont, New Jersey and Florida. The Rev. Horace Herrick, his brother-in-law and also a university trustee, had nominated Dennis for the award at the annual meeting of the Trustees of the University.[8] The honorary degree acknowledged his work as an educator and inventor.

On February 16, 1869, Dennis received Patent no. 87082 for his "folding-card globe, described as, "A flexible, expansible and compressible geographical...globe when made of a series of quadrantal [quadrantile] triangles." In addition to his knowledge of geography, Dennis used the principles of geometry to create the collapsible globe. Elmer, who agreed to pay the $100 for Dennis' patent application, also applied for his own inventions at nearly the same time. The following month, on March 23, 1869, Elmer patented "wire for shoe-pegs," followed by a patent with Louis Goddu on November 23 for a "machine for nailing shoe-soles with wire."[9] Elmer and an associate also invented a sewing machine to sew leather with a waxed thread. He was considered a pioneer in the shoe trade with inventions that revolutionized the business. He was also known as" the best wholesale auctioneer in Boston."[10]

Dennis created at least two versions of Townsend's Folding Globe. The first used an external stand to hold it open. In the second version, the

---

8 University of Vermont Trustees. *Annual Meeting Minutes*, August 5, 1868; *Burlington Free Press*, August 8, 1868.

9 U.S. House of Representatives, 41st Congress, 2d Session. *Annual Report of the Commissioner of Patents for the Year 1869*, Vol. 1 [Washington, Government Printing Office, 1871]. Dennis' and Elmer's inventions appeared in the same issue.

10 Townsend F.T. *Autobiography*, 14 and Meacham 14.

globe had an internal mechanism that held it open with rings positioned at both poles, allowing for expanding and collapsing the globe. All twelve paper sections of the globe were interconnected so that it lay flat when collapsed.

Producing and Promoting the Folding Globe

With the approval of his invention, Dennis had created a product that needed to be manufactured, priced, promoted, reviewed, and distributed to schools and homes. To be successful, he had to develop new skills in business that encompassed financing, advertising, licensing, contacts, and selling in order to turn a profit.

In the village of Felchville, fabricating the globe became a family enterprise. The invention was a source of pride for the family. In addition to the sisters, brother Buren was involved in the manufacturing. Rev. Horace Herrick, Aurelia's husband, became the recipient of thirty-six folding globes, licensed as an agent to sell them. With manufacturing costs at forty cents per globe, Dennis proposed that the globes could sell at retail for $1.50 each and at $12.00 per two dozen to schools. He would keep a few cents above cost and Rev. Herrick would retain the remainder of profit.[11] Herrick promoted the globes to such an extent that a Vermont newspaper mistakenly attributed its invention to him! *The Vermont Chronicle*, under "Windsor County Items." printed a retraction on April 24, 1869, proclaiming,

> We learn that D. Townsend of Felchville, recently from California, is the inventor and patentee of the folding globe, referred to in our last as the invention of Rev. H. Herrick of Wolcott—Mr. Herrick has been exhibiting a model of the globe but is he not the inventor. The globes are to be manufactured in Felchville in this county....We have had the pleasure of a glimpse of the model in the hand of the inventor and can say it looks well. We presume the public will soon be notified by the usual advertisements.[12]

Dennis had initially arranged with a lithographer in Boston to engrave the maps. Later, he spent three weeks of tough negotiations with George Savage in New York to have the "maps and covers made at lowest pric-

11 Meacham *Index: Dennis Townsend (D.T.)*, summary of May 26, 1869 letter.
12 *Vermont Chronicle*, Bellows Falls, Vermont, April 24, 1869. On May 1, 1869, another retraction was printed in the same newspaper under "Lamoille County," where Rev. Herrick clarified, "His brother-in-law Dennis Townsend, is the patentee and they will soon be on the market."

es." Savage became his sole agent, except for the New England region. The retail price for the globes was set at $1.25.

Aurelia enthusiastically wrote on May 31, 1869, "The more I examine it [the globe], the more surprised I am that a brother of ours should be able to accomplish such a thing...I find [that] men and women of the most intelligence are highly pleased and regard it as a success." Dennis' younger sister, Isabelle Waterman, who lived in Keokuk, Iowa, and her husband, Henry Waterman also helped to promote the globe. After they received a globe sent by Dennis, Henry brought it to the editor of the local newspaper, "who thought that Dennis had a hit this time. I got him to mention it in his editorials & also to copy the article from the *Teacher*...I shall take the Globe to K [Keokuk] & put it in the window at the Book Store."[13] Elmer praised Dennis with a p.s. in a letter to his mother, "I think Dennis has a splendid thing in the <u>Globe</u>."[14]

Dennis publicized and promoted his invention at schools, teacher's institutes, and in magazines. A flyer advertising the globe contained several favorable testimonials including the *Massachusetts Teacher* and the *Amador Ledger Dispatch,* which covered Amador County, Dennis' California home. The *LaMoille Newsdealer* of Vermont proclaimed, "It seems to be a triumph of ingenuity. We are certain that teachers and scholars will hail it with the greatest delight." The invention received an endorsement from *Scientific American* in its February 26, 1870 issue.[15]

> This is a novel and ingenious invention and publication, designed to place a cheap and convenient substitute for the revolving globe....When it is desired to see it [expand] by drawing upon small rings inserted at the poles, the whole assumes the globular form presenting to view, seas, mountains, continents, and other geographical features of the globe.

Walton's Vermont Register & Farmer's Almanac for 1870 advertised the globe, "Beautiful, cheap, and durable, it is fitted to supply a generally prevalent want....Parents cannot find a more acceptable and useful holiday present for their children. Do not fail to adorn your Christmas trees with the globe....Every child should have his or her own globe, available

---

13 Henry Waterman to Eliza Townsend, Keokuk, Iowa, March 16, 1869, VHS, MSC 133:10.
14 Elmer Townsend to Hannah Bigelow Townsend, Boston, January 10, 1870. VHS, MSC 133.3.
15 *Scientific American*, Vol. 22, number 9, February 26, 1870, 10 under Patent Office Decisions. *Internet Archive.*

for $1.00 with a portfolio or $1.25 when varnished, with a portfolio and key."

Ever the teacher, Dennis had written a twenty-four page booklet that accompanied his folding globe. *Townsend's Folding Globe Lessons*, published in 1870,[16] "designed especially for family instruction and the use of classes in the schools." The booklet frontispiece sported an endorsement from the Governor of Vermont and President of the State Board of Education, "admirably adapted for family instruction, and the use of classes in our Common Schools." Ten lessons detailed in 24 pages comprised questions and answers dealing with Planet Earth: its shape, land and water divisions, latitude, longitude, points of the compass and directional relationship of one place to another; axis, poles, meridians, tropics, polar circles, etc.

In the 21st century, students have access to devices such as GPS and digital maps, but in Townsend's time all this information had to be learned in school. His lessons aimed at creating understanding by correlating information with specific points on the globe, represented by letters and numbers. An accompanying key linked the numbered areas to the various features. In the Preface to the booklet, Dennis advised,

> Let the children be exercised—let them *play globe*—until they become familiar with the fundamental facts here presented, and they will *then* be well prepared to take up with profit the first book of any good series of geographies. To start right, then, we urge the importance of globe lessons to precede the primary geography.

Financing the Globe business

It is very likely that Dennis expected Elmer, his successful businessman brother, to provide the capital for producing the globe. But although Elmer was encouraging, he was occupied with his own business, the support of Eliza and Susan, plus his health was beginning to decline. He contributed some of financing and also his sisters pitched in. By December 1869, Dennis owed $1,300 to Elmer, Aurelia, and Susan. Elmer wrote a few months later to his sister [probably Susan], "Enclosed you have $100, $50 of which hand to Dennis for his use & keep $50 for the family. I am not very well. Dennis in his Globe I am satisfied has got a valuable invention and if he manages it well must make money out of it."[17]

16 vermonthistory.org/documents/digital/TownsendsFoldingGlobeLessons.pdf
17 Elmer Townsend to sister [name not specified], Boston, February 18, 1870. VHS MSC 133:3. Elmer died the following year on April 13, 1871.

The next year, Dennis proposed that Buren and Susan devote their whole time to the business, sharing net gains in other states with George Savage, paying Dennis a royalty on all globes sold in New England while keeping the net. On the Pacific Coast Dennis would take a royalty and share sales with Savage.[18] Potential sales were thus projected to occur on a national scale with siblings covering New England and other states, while California and the Pacific coast would be under Dennis' sole purview.

Dennis may have asked his wife in Fiddletown to join him early on in 1868 because Lizzy wrote to one of the sisters that October 18 that she couldn't come East to live because she owes her life to California's climate. "Mr. Townsend's health would be good any place, if he would use judgement and not overtax his mind so much. We are both alike; he studies himself to death and I work myself to death." Her assessment verified that Dennis was consumed by his profession and his invention.

Dennis left his immediate family behind for two years to realize his vision of the globe. It was not until summer of 1870 that Lizzy joined the Townsend family in Vermont, after struggling alone to care for and support her children. However, travel had improved. With the completion of the transcontinental railroad, she was now able to take the train from Sacramento to cross the continent, a much faster and easier journey than by sea. The children, Emma and Dennis, Jr. would likely have accompanied her, although this is not mentioned in any of the family correspondence. After staying in Vermont, Lizzy took the opportunity the following year to travel to her hometown of Carrollton, Illinois to visit family and friends, including a married sister, Mary Ann Williams.

Sometime in 1871, Dennis must have briefly journeyed alone to California to attend the California Teachers' Institute of that year. As reported in the July, 1871-June 1872 issue of *The California Teacher*, he "came forward" to present his globe as the best way to teach geography. A review in the same magazine concluded that, "A cheap globe has long been a desideratum among educators. In this Folding Globe, Mr. Townsend has supplied the long-felt want in a manner that entitles him to commendation and thanks....The *ingeniousness* of the arrangement in wonderful. The inventor is a California teacher, residing at Fiddletown, Amador County, hailing originally from the land of sharp intellects... Old Vermont. We again take occasion to call favorable attention to this

---

18 Meacham *Index: D.T.*

Globe."[19]Although one member of the Institute's audience objected to this method because "it represented an unnatural transformation of the earth,"[20] the other teachers voted to recommend the use and adoption of the Folding Globe.

In June 1871, Dennis' sister Isabelle Waterman in Keokuk, Iowa awaited his arrival. He had written to her husband Henry that he hoped to find employment. She observed, "[He] has not had good success in the agency he has undertaken. We feel very sorry for him & shall aid him all in our power to procure a situation of some kind. We expect him here soon. I wish he was able to go with the globe business. Wish we were able to help him. He thinks money might be made in it. I feel very sad for his misfortunes. He is a dear good brother."[21]

For a time, the business helped to support Eliza and Susan [after Elmer died] in Felchville,[22] but many more globes had to be sold to gain a profit. After spending almost four years away, Dennis began to contemplate permanently returning to California. Writing to the Felchville family on October 7, 1871, he stated, "I would like not to be separated from you but I pray to be delivered from that country and climate [of Vermont]... I have been repeatedly called foolish in leaving Felchville and I suppose you feel that I am ungrateful for favors already conferred." In another letter sent to Aurelia and Susan, he affirmed it was "not necessary to success of the globe that I should be in New England. Buren can manufacture as well as I."[23] He was more than ready to abandon the cold regions of Vermont and also shift responsibility for the globe production. His heart was now in California. The Golden State, with its beneficent climate was calling to him.

---

19 The California Teacher (July 1871-June 1872): Internet Archive.
20 Probably meaning the transformation from a two-dimensional flat map to the three-dimensional globe.
21 Isabelle Waterman to Eliza Townsend, June 4, 1871 with addition 4 days later. There is no mention in letters from Isabelle about their children accompanying them.
22 Meacham, 23.
23 Meacham *Index:D.T.* Notes do not specify the recipient for the letter of October 7, likely directed to the Vermont family. No date is given for the letter to Aurelia and Susan. It is not clear where Dennis was when he wrote these letters. Probably he was in Keokuk, Iowa, intending to head west to California.

Letters: 1868

Felchville, Dec. 5th, 1868

Dear Sisters Susan and Aurelia,[1]

Yours of the 1st has come to hand. I have concluded to commence work here.

Mother rec'd a letter from Elmer a few days ago in which he proposed that suitable improvements should be made in the house here for your accommodation and that you should all live together and that the globe making could be carried on here.

Mother was pleased with the idea and thought it would be best for all. She wrote to Elmer to that effect.

Elmer says that he shall do all he can to make things agreeable. He says that it should cost me nothing while I stay. Noble fellow! I feel that I am entirely undeserving of such kindness and generosity and ardently pray that I may be successful so that I may make full returns—if not to him to some other deserving ones in need.

I shall go to Springfield a week or two—will write to you from there. The cutting machine is nearly done.

Susan, you need not hurry about coming for I doubt whether I shall be ready to manufacture in less than six weeks or two months. Think I shall have to go to Boston again to secure explanations to the lithographer, for you are aware that it is necessary that the engraving should be done with exactness. Elmer tells me to go slow and sure in starting my invention.

Rec'd a letter from my little girl and my little boy—They are all well and the children are going to school.

Glad to learn that the globe meets the approval of teachers.

Your affectionate Br

Dennis Townsend

---

1 Susan was visiting Aurelia at her home in Wolcott, Vermont.

Felchville, December 17, 1868

My dear Sisters, [Aurelia and Susan]

Your enclosure with a letter to Eliza was rec'd several days ago. I have delayed replying on account of being engaged in studying yet an improvement in the arrangement for expanding the globe. I have got the thing now about to my notion. The spring is more simple and more easily made and is fixed to remain always attached to the globe.

I expect my cutting and folding machines to be ready in a few days when I hope to get up a globe by them and proceed with the drawing. I thought best to have Gilman[2] make a folder as I can more easily communicate with him in regard to it than I could with Brother Herrick and could more readily have any needed change made in it, if it should not work just right. I am no less grateful to him for his kind and generous offer to get up that machine for me.

I am overwhelmed with kindness on every side. I am in good health and well provided for in every particular. Graham is the staff of life with me.[3] I sleep in the parlor where I am now writing by a good fire in a snug little stove. I sleep in a woolen nightgown which mother has provided, that covers me from top to toe. I am wearing one of the most comfortable of flannel shirts made by Eliza. Rubbers incase my feet when I go out. The heated stove warms my bed before I retire.[4] I bathe by a good fire. Mother has provided me with thick drawers and a pair of excellent woolen mittens.

I have coats enough for a Greenlander. Time fails me to enumerate my comforts. If there is anything else you imagined that I require just suppose that I have it and my care is described.

I am very grateful to Br. H. [Herrick] and you for the offer of a home this winter, besides the very great and valuable favors you have bestowed upon me. Thank you Susan for the offer of your railroad stock but I hope that I shall not need it. Let it rest where it is until an emergency call for it.

---

2 Townsend, F.T. *Autobiography*, 20. Alstyne and his brother-in-law Gilman eventually became partners. The machine shop, known as Gilman & Townsend, later manufactured shoe lace machines, probably invented by Elmer Townsend.

3 Graham flour is a course-ground type of whole wheat that was advocated by Sylvester Graham as a healthy alternative to white bread since it contains wheat germ and bran.

4 Dennis' handwriting becomes scrawling with heavier ink at this point. By the last paragraph, it gets larger and more urgent, indicating anxiety.

Don't distress yourselves any more about me but look to your-selves. I think the river of sympathy should reverse its course and flow from me awhile. I don't want to brag but I wouldn't be afraid to bet two to one that my health is better than yours now and I don't "<u>shiver</u>" half as much. Saw the new moon over my left shoulder, but I am sorry that I have told you of [this] for I am afraid that it will destroy your peace of mind.[5]

Tell me your news.
Very affectionately

Dennis Townsend

VHS MSC133: 7

---

5 www.superstitionsof.com/superstitions-of-the-moon.htm. The Moon seen over the right shoulder brings good luck; the Moon seen over the left shoulder brings bad luck.

Figure 23. Felchville, North, 1895: *Reading Historical Society*

Figure 24. Felchville, South, 1895: *Reading Historical Society*

Figure 25. Townsend's Patent Folding Globe. *Courtesy David Rumsey Map Collection at Stanford University Libraries, David Rumsey Map Center, Stanford Libraries https://purl.stanford.edu/td076cv5406*

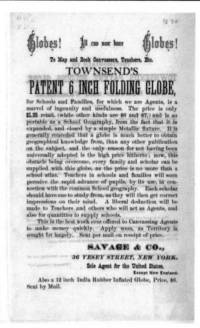

Figure 26. Ad for canvassers to sell Folding Globe : *Vermont Historical Society*

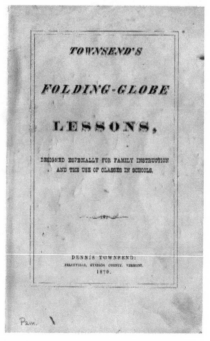

Figure 27. Townsend's Folding Globe Lessons: *Vermont Historical Society*

CHAPTER 6

Return to California, Last Days

During the latter part of 1871, Dennis and family returned to Fiddletown, but no letters allude to how or when they arrived in Fiddletown. They may have taken trains from Iowa to the transcontinental railroad starting point in Omaha, Nebraska, and from there to Sacramento.[1] In a July 1872 letter to Susan, Dennis called the Sierra Nevada foothills, "God's Country," delighting in the weather and the bounty of summer fruit of apples, peaches, nectarines, apricots, pears, grapes. In late December of 1872, he asserted, "Teaching is the best thing that I can do for a living at present....I walk nearly two miles to school which affords me plenty of healthy exercise....After a year's teaching, my health is quite as good, if not better, than when I commenced after our return....As to the globe, I must trust luck and future developments."[2] Was he exaggerating about his improving health to reassure his family? His sister Isabelle noted to Susan a few months earlier, "Poor brother Dennis. I often think of him with his ill health. Does Lizzie write you how her health is?"[3]

Despite all the accolades and endorsement of his invention, once Dennis returned to California, he could not devote his time to promoting and selling his creation. He needed to earn a living by resuming teaching public school. He had struggled in earlier years with $100 monthly wage. This time around he was paid less, only $80 a month, reflecting the pervasive low salaries of teachers. Dennis and his family could barely survive on such a low salary. By the 1870s, the number of women teachers had greatly expanded to become the majority across the country. Their salaries were even less than men's.[4]

---

1 Council Bluffs, Iowa, was designated by President Lincoln as eastern terminus of the transcontinental railroad, but that connection was delayed until a bridge was built over the Missouri River joining Council Bluffs and Omaha in 1872.
2 Meacham *Index: D.T.* does not refer to letters in late 1871 or the first half of 1872. Quotes are reproduced from portions of letters written July 21 and December 29, 1872.
3 Isabelle Waterman to Susan Fay, September, 1872, MSC 133:10. Transcribed by Leslee Mayo.
4 Weiler, *Country Schoolwomen*, 37-40. The differential in salaries was less in California than in other parts of the country. A movement in 1872 for equal pay for equal work resulted in 1874 California legislation to ban pay discrimination against women teachers. Women teachers were often required to be unmarried.

Dennis was teaching in two unnamed adjoining school districts, six months in each. They were a distance from Fiddletown, requiring him to board away from home.[5] It was common practice for teachers to board with a student's family. This meant an extra expense plus separation from his family for week days during the teaching year, leaving Lizzy in charge of the children and the daily household chores. With teaching commitments for twelve months of the year, Dennis had no time left for a summer vacation or for visits to other locations to advance sales of his invention.

Dennis had realized his dream of creating the collapsible folding globe, an achievement of a lifetime. He had hoped that his invention would bring prosperity, recognition, and widespread adoption in schools throughout the nation. The expectations were high, but it became clear that the folding globe would not bring in enough revenue to sustain Dennis' immediate family, let alone become profitable. He continued to be in debt to Aurelia and Susan, suggesting to them that money coming in from globe sales could be deducted and applied to what he owed. He was prepared to pay interest on the notes. His descendant, Bessie Meacham, observed after reading all the family letters,[6]

> The members of the family always tried to help one another financially as they were able. They seemed to give notes for all money received, but the interest and principal seems to have been paid irregularly and sometimes not at all. But that was because of financial inability, not design.

Dennis confessed in a letter on May 18, 1873 to the Felchville family that his work teaching school consumed all his energy, preventing him from promoting the globe. Lizzy had taken on dressmaking to help the family survive financially. As a debtor and as a hard working underpaid teacher, Dennis was under great pressure, so much pressure that he may have cracked under the strain.

That fall, Dennis became seriously debilitated, first breaking down physically and then mentally. After his death, Lizzy revealed in letter to Eliza that the illness began in October, 1873 with a pain in the head and bowels; a month later he "went completely out of his head." He began to wander away from home, once as far as nine miles away. After his behavior became increasingly unpredictable with irrational outbursts, she

---

5 Meacham *Index: D.T.* The two adjoining districts were possibly in neighboring El Dorado County.
6 Meacham, *Chronicle*, 26-7.

sought medical help.[7] On December 8, Dr. William Pitt examined Dennis in Jackson, deeming him "an insane person."[8] The next day, he was transported and confined to the Stockton State Hospital, otherwise called the Insane Asylum of California. As reported in the *Amador Dispatch* on December 13, 1873:

> Mr. Dennis Townsend, of Fiddletown, was arrested and brought to town last week on a charge on insanity, and on Monday last, was examined before Judge Adams, and ordered sent to the asylum at Stockton. Mr. Townsend was a man of good education, and was at one time, we believe, elected as Superintendent of Schools of this county. His insanity is supposed to have been caused from overtaxing his brain upon the subject of a new globe map which he invented several years ago, and which is said to have been a very useful and invention, but did not meet his expectation in a financial point of view.

The Commitment Register to the Stockton State Hospital provided a detailed description of his illness and the behavior that preceded it.

> Committed by the Hon. A. Adams District Judge of the 11th Judicial District of the State of California embracing the County of Amador. Complainant L.J. Hulot, Witnesses Elizabeth Townsend and Jos. A. Robinson. Examining Physicians Drs. Charles Boarman and William Pitt.

> Age 56 years. Native of Vermont. Married with two children the youngest 10 years of age. Last from the State of Illinois. In the State of California for 21 years. Occupation School Teacher. Evidence of the presence of Insanity. Strange and violent language and violent conduct generally. He is of a homicidal and suicidal disposition. This is a recent case. His attack first appeared about 4 weeks ago. This is the first attack. The disease is increasing. He has rational intervals no particular times. As a teacher he thinks of a Globe of his own invention for the use of common schools. Dangerous to be at large, owing to his family and friends fearing personal violence; and the community in which he lives fear him as an incendiary. At times there is a fear of his injuring his best friends. No disposition to injure any one in particular. A disposition to destroy any thing that comes within his reach, when in one of his paroxysms. One of his brothers was insane. His health has improved since the attack of insanity. Supposed Cause of insanity: Sickness Class: Mania.[9]

7 Meacham *Index: D.T.* Elizabeth Townsend to Eliza Townsend, March 27, 1874.
8 Amador County, *Bill*, Dr. William Pitt, filed December 8, 1873, Amador County Archives.
9 California Department of Mental Hygiene-Stockton State Hospital Records. *Commitment Register*, R320 series 2, California State Archives, Office of the Secretary of State, Sacramento, California. Record #6048 transcribed by Liz Allenby. Dennis'

The Stockton State Hospital admitted Dennis on December 9, 1873 and discharged him on February 20, 1874, after slightly more than two months of confinement. On February 21, 1874, one day after being released to his wife, Dennis Townsend died. He was 57 years old, leaving behind Lizzy, daughter Mary Emma age 17, and son, Dennis, Jr., age 13. His death so soon after leaving the hospital is baffling. Why was he released then, if his health was precarious? Was his mental condition stabilized, but his body failing? Did Lizzy ask to have him released?

In her petition to the Amador County Probate Court on March 24, 1874, Elizabeth "Lizzy" Townsend stated that Dennis died in Stockton in San Joaquin County. However, there are no records of his death in that county.[10] Townsend's death is entered in the Amador County Register of Death for February 21, 1874 with the cause of death listed as consumption, his body examined by the physician or coroner who signed the register. He must have died in Fiddletown or Jackson. Lizzy described that he almost died in her arms. "It is hard to give him up although I know he is in a better world."[11]

Dennis had a history of respiratory illness, but not of having tuberculosis. During the periodic bouts of respiratory illness that he experienced throughout the years, his outlook became morose and he had premonitions of early death. In the letter written to Eliza one month after his death Lizzy wrote that prior to his hospital admission, "the only diagnosis was of inflammation of the brain, and of bowels;" the Stockton State Hospital identified "mania" as his reason for institutionalization. How would these maladies be described today? At the time, psychology and the study of mental illness were in their infancy. From the letters, Dennis revealed an intense and obsessive personality that could swing between elation and depression.

His son, Dennis Townsend, Jr. wrote to his cousin Willie about the death of his father.

> ...I have sad news to write to you. My pa died on the 21st of February, he was sick five months and was in the insane asylum 2 months but did not die in the asylum. The Dr [doctor's] reason given for his insanity was by over studding [studying]. Ma was with pa most of the time. Pa was in his right mind for two weeks before he died. Ma is going to write as soon as

brother Albert, who died early, was an alcoholic and often in debt.

10 The name Dennis Townsend did not appear in San Joaquin County Recorder's Office search of *Death Certificates* or the San Joaquin County Public Library *Obituary Index, 1850-1991*.

11 Meacham *Index: D.T.* Elizabeth Townsend to Eliza Townsend, March 27, 1874.

she feels better.[12]

Dennis' family had anticipated his death. Isabelle Waterman enclosed a copy of the above letter to one of her sisters, writing in its margins, "I used to think sometimes that Lizzie felt far more than she was willing to express. We received this letter from Dennis the same mail with your postal card informing us of his father's death. I had been fearing we might hear it at any time. If Lizzie's health continues poor I do not see how she is going to get along without help from some source..."[13]

Buren, who Dennis hoped would manufacture the globe, wrote to his mother and sisters in Felchville from Worcester, Massachusetts on March 23, 1874:

> Yours of the 3rd and Postal card of the 10th are red [read] with the sad news of dear Bro. Dennis death: I have been afraid we should not have him with us long: probably you remember that as he was playing on Father's violin the night before he left Felchville [he] remarked that he would never play on it again: but my fear was not caused by that remark but by his liability to an attack similar to the one he had not long since. Why didn't we hear of his sickness which lasted 4 months? What can reconcile us to our loss but the hope that "what is our loss is his gain." In what circumstances did he leave his family? Have Aurelia and Susan been paid for what they did to get the Globe started? I wish the Globe would yet benefit his family, and become a blessing to the World.[14]

Dennis Townsend died without a will. His widow, Lizzy, was left to administer his estate in probate court. The assets recorded in the estate inventory were paltry, consisting of their house in Fiddletown, sparse furniture including a sewing machine, 500 globes, and the patent rights to the folding globe.[15] Dennis had no debts in Amador County nor was it noted that he owned additional property, such as the lot in Volcano. Lizzy's brother-in-law, Mr. Edward Kingsley pitched in to pay for funeral expenses without expecting payment in return. But with the family debt still outstanding, Lizzy felt obligated to pay Susan for her loan. For years she kept in contact with Susan and her daughter Minnie, always hoping to sell the globe business as compensation.[16]

12 Dennis Townsend, Jr. to William Waterman, March 6, 1874, VHS MSC 133:10
13 Isabelle Waterman note appended to above copied letter, date or recipient not identified.
14 Van Buren Townsend to Hannah Bigelow Townsend and Family, Worcester, Mass., March 23, 1874, VHS MSC: 15.
15 Amador County Probate Court, Probate *Record 303*, 1876, Amador County Archives.
16 Meacham *Index: D.T.* Lizzy Townsend to Susan Fay, May 3, 1874.

Coda

In the Fiddletown public cemetery across the road from the Fiddletown Schoolhouse, a prominent obelisk tombstone stands under the shade of a huge oak tree marking the grave of Dennis Townsend, Fiddletown's first postmaster and first teacher.

Settling in California during its early development in the 1850s, he made the transition from Vermont to California, reveling in the comparatively mild climate, its health benefits, abundance and potential. His letters from California remain an important first-hand record of the experiences and impressions of an educator who contributed to the evolving society in the Far West during a period of great change in the state and the nation.

A most eloquent tribute to Dennis appeared in the 1881 *History of Amador County, California* written by Jesse D. Mason, who likely knew him.

> Few men were more devoted to their profession than Dennis Townsend. Coming to California when gold-hunting was the sole object with most men, his educational feelings were aroused by the sight of the children growing up untaught. Leaving the making of a fortune out of the question, he adopted the profession of a teacher, at a time that it meant inevitable poverty and sacrifice, which profession he followed during his life, or, until the arduous duties ruined his health and mind. If we measure men's wealth by the accumulation of gold, he died poor; if by the love of thousands of human beings, who have modeled their lives after his instruction, and hold his memory in veneration, he died one of the wealthiest men in the country. He was the inventor of the folding globe, by which the study of geography has been greatly simplified.[17]

Townsend's Folding Globe made tangible the continents, poles and seas of our round planet Earth, opening up a new understanding of our world. The folding globe of Dennis Townsend resides in the Norman B. Leventhal Map & Education Center at the Boston Public Library; the David Rumsey Map Collection at Stanford University Libraries, the Vermont Historical Society; and the Norwich [Vt.] Historical Society. The folding globe is exhibited at the California State Capitol and the Amador County Museum. A search on the Web for *Townsend's Patent Folding Globe* yields images and detailed information about the properties of the

---

17 Mason, 225.

globe. This "fascinating little piece of global wizardry" has also become a collectible. Bookdealers on the Internet list *Townsend's Folding Globe* either for sale or sold. In 2022, a copy of the folding globe, along with Townsend's booklet of Lessons, is available through an antiquarian book dealer for $4,500.[18]

18 TOWNSEND'S PATENT FOLDING GLOBE | David Townsend (bartlebysbooks.com)

Figure 28. Townsend Family in Felchville, circa 1876: *Vermont Historical Society*

Figure 29. Townsend burial monument in Fiddletown Public Cemetery

Epilogue

After her husband died, Elizabeth Townsend or Lizzy struggled to survive on sales of the folding globes, barely able to cover household expenses. In 1875, she rented her sister Margaret Kingsley's boarding house in Ione, the Veranda Hotel, for a month. Although income there was paltry since few boarders paid, it may have given her the notion to start her own hotel or boarding house in Fiddletown. It is not known how Lizzy acquired four contiguous properties on Main Street or the funds to build the St. Charles Hotel.[1] The hotel was on the north side of Main Street, slightly east of the long established U.S. Hotel across the road. In the 1880s, Lizzy made various improvements to her hotel by painting, rebuilding the front and renovating "inside and out" in 1886."[2] That year, besides refurbishing the hotel, she acquired an irregular piece of land known as Bage Ranch, about 1 ½ miles west of Fiddletown.

Meanwhile, in July 1877, daughter Mary Emma married George Love, a teamster formerly from Ione. In the 1880 Census they and their three children were living in the hotel with Lizzy, son Dennis Jr., and two boarders. Mary Emma [known as Emma] gave birth to five more children between 1882 and 1890. Twenty years later in 1900 Lizzy at age 72 continued to be in charge of the hotel, with both her son (a day laborer) and daughter living with her as well as six grandchildren.[3] That year George Love resided in a boarding house in Sutter Creek. He was still working as a teamster but had been unemployed for six months.

Into her late years, Lizzy functioned as the mainstay for her children and grandchildren. Lizzy had held on to the property in Volcano, where she and Dennis briefly resided in a house that was destroyed by fire in 1865. She sold that lot in 1898.[4]

Lizzy's son, Dennis Townsend Jr. spent his life in Fiddletown. His passion was placer gold mining. In 1883, he and a partner sold a claim for

1 The Townsend home was originally Lot 13, Block 6. At the time of her death, Lizzy owned lots 13, 14, 15, and 16 in Block 6 in Fiddletown.
2 *Amador Ledger*, March 3, 1883; September 8, 1883, and August 21, 1886.
3 Household data is based on the 1880 and 1900; the Census for 1890 is missing. The oldest grandson, Elmer F. Love (in the 1880 Census listed as Frank E.) was age 22 and also a day laborer in 1900. Two twin sisters, Carrie E. and Cynthia M. Love born in 1879 were no longer in Fiddletown by 1900 and have not been traced. The other grandchildren living with Lizzy were between 10 and 17 years old.
4 *Amador County Deeds*, March 19, 1898, Book 16, Page 8. The property at Lot 3, Block 9 in Volcano was sold to Rose Schunck for $10.00.

$300 to Chinese miners, who later successfully extracted $30,000 in gold from the claim.[5] Dennis operated a saloon on Main Street that was nearly destroyed during a fire in 1895. Through the years, he worked for several small placer mines in the vicinity. Dennis was active in community life; however he remained single.

In May 1902, a fire started at the U.S. Hotel, spreading across the street to the St. Charles Hotel. The newspaper did not have the details, but was "informed that both hotels, two saloons, a drug store and three dwellings, with all their contents, were destroyed." The fire devastated the town, which was already struggling[6] and it must have been shattering to Lizzy and her family. Locals tried to help her later in the month by giving a benefit dance in town. Family and friends sent clothes and money. By this time her sisters, Margaret Kingsley of Ione and Jane Perry of Rio Vista, California, and their spouses had died. Her brother, Dr. John Ray who lived in Redondo Beach, visited Fiddletown to help her during an illness in 1906. Lizzy kept in touch with the Felchville family—first corresponding with Susan Townsend Fay, and then with Susan's daughter, Minnie Fay, after Susan died.

By 1903 her house was partially rebuilt, enough so she and daughter Mary Emma could accommodate boarders.[7] The Census of 1910 showed Lizzy, 81, as head of the family, living together with son Dennis, daughter Mary Emma and her husband, three sons and daughter Maggie [Margaret].

Hardship continued when on December 20, 1911, Lizzy's son-in-law George Love died at the age of sixty, after a two year illness, leaving behind five of the nine children. The eldest, Elmer F. Love had relocated to Loomis, California, but Edward, Dennis, Raymond and Maggie remained in Fiddletown. In 1915, Maggie Love married Hugh D. Upton from the nearby Shenandoah Valley. There were no children from that union, or from the remaining three sons of Mary Emma and George.[8]

5 *Amador Ledger*, February 17, 1883, March 3, 1916. Located in the American Flat mining area, the claim may have been on the Loafer Flat land where his father, Dennis Townsend, filed a preemption claim.

6 *Amador Ledger*, May 9, 1902, "Big Fire at Oleta" and May 23, 1902. The name of Fiddletown was changed in 1878 to Oleta, which held until 1932 when it reverted back to Fiddletown.

7 Meacham *Index: D.T.* A reference to a January 24, 1910 letter from Lizzy to Minnie states that the house was not finished inside. No mention is made to the hotel being reconstructed.

8 [Dixon, Elsie], The *Shenandoah Valley Area of Amador County, California* (Sacramento, 1976), 261, 267, 358. Dixon and the *Amador Ledger* list 9 children from

Elizabeth Ray Townsend died at age eighty-nine on February 10, 1917, leaving behind her children and grandchildren. She willed her property to Mary Emma and Dennis Jr., but a few months later both siblings sold the four parcels in Fiddletown to Mary Emma's oldest son, Elmer F. Love.[9] Mary Emma Townsend Love died July 20, 1925, likely buried besides her husband in the Fiddletown IOOF Cemetery, both in unmarked graves. Dennis Jr. died September 24, 1938 at age seventy-seven. Presumably, he and his mother are buried in unmarked graves in the Fiddletown Cemetery close to the monument of Dennis Townsend.

St. Charles Hotel survived Lizzy, although no information has been found on its condition after the fire. The property was inherited by the Townsend grandson Elmer F. Love, who in 1930 lived on his own farm in Placer County, along with his wife and two daughters. In July 1935, the local newspaper announced that he had sold the "Old St. Charles Hotel formerly owned by the late Mrs. Elizabeth Townsend," to Arthur Lachapelle. That September, Mr. Lachapelle tore down the St. Charles Hotel, with plans to build a few homes on its lot.[10]

The Townsend Siblings

Several of Dennis' siblings had preceded him in death. From the same birth mother, Susannah Smith, sons Elmer, Orson, Albert, Alfred, William had died, leaving Dennis, Susan and Aurelia still living. The remaining siblings continued to correspond with each other sharing their respective activities, family visits, life events and developments with work, travel, family illness, children and grandchildren. None of them ever ventured as far away as California. In the 1870s, the youngest, Marquis, settled in Conneaut, Ohio; Torrey relocated from his farm in Dutch Creek to Clay, Iowa, twelve miles distant. Isabelle and her husband moved from Keokuk, Iowa to Milford, Nebraska after experiencing a business loss. Aurelia and her husband visited family in the "West," staying for a couple of years in Nebraska, before heading east again to eventually settle in Felchville. Alstyne continued to live in Springfield, Vermont, and Velette and Buren remained in Worchester, Massachusetts. Buren had returned

---

the marriage, including Frank E. and Elmer F., likely the same person. The 1910 and 1920 Census revealed serious learning disabilities with the three younger boys, all unable to write, two unable to read.

9 Amador County *Deeds*, March 12, 1917 book 39, pg. 423 and June 8, 1917, book 40, pg. 41.

10 *Amador Ledger and Amador Record*, July 18, 1935 and September 19, 1935.

there for several years after an unsuccessful venture in Florida, but in 1886 relocated to his preferred destination near Tampa. At some point, Isabelle and her family moved again, to join their son in Mapleton, Kansas, where he operated a drug store. [11]

Felchville Vermont continued to be the family nexus where mother Hannah Bigelow Townsend lived with Susan, Minnie and Eliza. First Susan passed away in July, 1879. By 1880, Aurelia and Horace Herrick resided in the same household. At age ninety, Hannah died on February 26, 1884. As Bessie Meacham wrote in her *Chronicle*, "They all [her children] speak of the admiration, respect and love they had for her and her lasting influence on their lives. She kept in close touch with them through innumerable letters, and it was she who preserved the letters from which this history has been compiled." The practice of retaining family letters continued after Hannah died. Aurelia and her husband both passed on in 1891. In 1900, Torrey visited Marquis, Velette, and Eliza, observing, "We four are the only ones left of our large family."[12] Minnie cared for Eliza until she died at age 90. Minnie continued to live in the family home, becoming the village librarian and operating a Sunday school.

It is thanks to Francis Torrey Townsend in Iowa and his descendants that the family archive has survived. Torrey became the first family historian by tracing the family genealogy in his *Autobiography*. His granddaughter Bessie Meacham took on the huge project to read, record, and compile the correspondence of the prolific letter writers in this large and affectionate family. By placing the letters with the Vermont Historical Society and the University of Texas, Austin, she ensured their long-term preservation and public access.

---

11 Meacham, 24-32. More detail about the siblings is given in the *Chronicle*.
12 Townsend, F.T., *Autobiography*, 53.

Figure 30. Dennis Townsend, Jr: *Courtesy Andrew Oliver-Rudis*

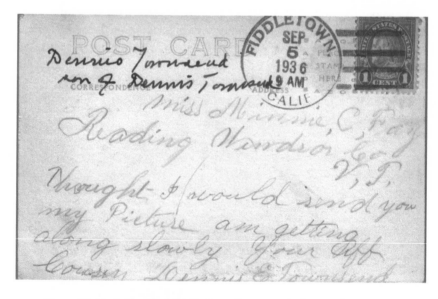

Figure 31. Post Card to Minnie Fay: *Courtesy Andrew Oliver-Rudis*

Figure 32. St. Charles Hotel in Fiddletown: *Amador County Archives*

Figure 33. Eliza and Marquis Townsend, Minnie Fay in Felchville home:
Courtesy, Reading Historical Society

Figure 34. Francis Torrey Townsend: *Courtesy, Reading Historical Society*

Figure 35. Eliza Townsend in Felchville: *Courtesy, Reading Historical Society*

146

Acknowledgments

Although discovery and transcription of the Townsend Family letters took place over many years, the writing and much of the research occurred during the Covid-19 pandemic in early 2020. Many libraries were in lockdown. Yet with the magic of the Internet, information was retrieved, email correspondence occurred, and documents and photographs were received.

Paul Carnahan, Librarian of the Leahy Library of the Vermont Historical Society was instrumental in helping me through the years, responding to my many questions, sending copies of the letters, verifying names, dates and other information in the manuscripts, scanning and providing links for Townsend materials, giving referrals for photographs, etc. Paul even had a volunteer peruse the letters of the Townsend siblings in 2012 for mention of Dennis, which he scanned. It is thanks to Paul and his volunteer, Mark, that those letters became available to me. In transcribing Dennis' letters, I encountered some words that were difficult to read. At Paul's request, Assistant Librarian Marjorie Strong did a great job in early 2019 deciphering the problem words. Paul retired this year after many years of providing excellent service. I wish him good health and fulfillment for this phase of his life. He may be amazed that my book has materialized at last!

Librarians and staff at the Dolph Briscoe Center for American History at the University of Texas in Austin were most accommodating. I learned from Reference Archivist Catherine Best that the Dennis Townsend papers were originally part of the Walter Prescott Webb papers before they were moved to their own collection. Aryn Glazier of Photo Services relayed photographs and images relating to Dennis Townsend in 2013 and 2022. I am especially grateful to Reference Archivist Erin Harbour, who during lockdown went onsite to the university library, where she examined and itemized all the Dennis Townsend manuscript letters in search of a missing letter. This was not an easy task because of poor legibility of the handwriting. Her search confirmed that all of the letters at the Dolph Briscoe Center were reproduced digitally by the Vermont Historical Society and that the missing letter is still missing.

Despite lack of face-to-face contact during the pandemic, several people assisted me from a distance. Through the Townsend Society of America, I was put in contact with Leslee Mayo, who is related to Isabelle Townsend Waterman, wife of her great-great-grandfather, Henry Waterman. Leslee obtained Isabelle's letters and transcribed all of them, covering 1862-1909. She also found that Dennis was a particularly interesting ancestor and proceeded to research his life. Leslee was very generous in sharing her transcriptions, her files on Dennis Townsend that included genealogical sheets, and her paper on the life of Dennis Townsend, held by the Townsend Society.

My thanks to Esther Allen, of the Reading Historical Society in Vermont, Mary Ellen of the Greene County Historical & Genealogical Society in Illinois, Tom Latham of the Eastford Historical Society in Connecticut, and Bev Lindemann, great-great-granddaughter of Francis Torrey and niece of Bessie Meacham. Bessie had lived in Eastford, CT and died on April 3, 1975.

Librarians and archivists, essential for any researcher, always rise to the challenge. Prudence Doherty, Librarian of the Silver Special Collections Library at the University of Vermont took the extra step to provide me with trustee and newspaper information. Elena Smith of the California State Library ably assisted me with finding maps and obtaining images. Teresa Guidi of the Amador County Archives provided scans of requested items during the lockdown; after libraries resumed partial services, Robin Ivanoff of the Amador County Library fact checked and obtained books for me on interlibrary loan.

In my journey to learn more about Dennis Townsend, Vermonter Charles T. Morrissey, towering figure in the field of oral history and retired Director and Consultant for the Oral History Project at Baylor College of Medicine in Houston, was the first to send me Townsend information from Vermont—also featuring Dennis Townsend on his Vermont radio program in 1999. Frank Tortorich, expert on the Carson River Route of the Emigrant Trail through the Sierra Nevada, set me on the right path for the route of the Carson Trail's Volcano Cut-off.

This book would not be what it is, if not for my friend, the historian Ava F. Kahn, author of *Jewish Voices of the California Gold Rush* and other books concerning the experience of Jews in the West. Excited about the content of the Dennis Townsend letters, Ava participated in every phase of the manuscript, pointing out the historical context, raising questions that prodded me to delve deeper into the life and times, scrutinizing the language, phrasing, organization, quality of information, and making suggestions for improving the content and expression. During these past three years, Ava acted as my best critic, editor, and cheerleader. I am deeply grateful to her for all her contributions and close involvement, encouragement, and patience.

I am very grateful that historian and retired museum curator James Nottage read my manuscript and wrote an edifying foreword, after finding that the "Townsend story is compelling and merits publication."

My thanks to Alice Kaiser and Sally Veauta, enthusiastic readers of the first completed version and friend Lois Johnson, whose continuing interest in this project spurred me onward.

Credit to spouses or partners, the most important person in one's life, always comes at the end of the acknowledgements. My husband, Dimitri, a superb writer himself, has again applied his technical wizardry to converting the manuscript into print. He designed the cover and book, integrated the different sections and illustrations, pruned and improved the index and spent many days overcoming software incompatibilities to bring the book into existence. I can never praise him enough for all he does to keep our household and farm functioning smoothly while rescuing me from computer gaffes.

Bibliography

Archival & Government Sources
Amador County Archives
Amador County, *"Petition of School Teachers of Amador County for an increase of Salary of County Superintendent."*
Amador County Probate Court, *Probate of Dennis Townsend, 1874.*
Amador County, *Tax Assessment Roll*, 1855 and 1856
Amador County Teacher's Institute applications and petition
Amador County Superintendent of School bills and claims
Amador County Recorder's Office
Amador County *Deeds* 1854-1934
Amador County, *Judges Certificates, Fiddletown and Volcano*
Amador County, *Register of Death*, 1874
California State Archives
California Department of Mental Hygiene-Stockton State Hospital Records. *Commitment Register*, R320 series 2. California State Archives, Office of the Secretary of State, Sacramento, California.
California State Land Office Records, R 388 [Series 12] [Box41]. *School Fund Apportionment Reports, Annual Census returns 1861-1869.* California State Archives, Office of the Secretary of State, Sacramento, California.
El Dorado County
Tax Assessment Role, 1854
Preemption Book [circa 1853]
San Joaquin County Recorder's Office
Death Certificates
University of Vermont Trustees. *Annual Meeting Minutes*, August 5, 1868.
U.S. Census of Population 1860-1930
U.S. House of Representatives, 41st Congress, 2d Session. *Annual Report of the Commissioner of Patents for the Year 1869*, Vol. 1. Washington, Government Printing Office, 1871.

Manuscripts, Diaries and Unpublished Papers
Bailey, Mary Stuart, "A Journal of Mary Stuart Bailey, April-October,

1852" in *Ho for California! Women's Overland Diaries from the Huntington Library*, edited and annotated by Sandra L. Myres. San Marino, Huntington Library, 1980.

Carvalho, Soloman Nunes. *Incidents of Travel and Adventure in the Far West with Colonel Frémont's Last Expedition*. Lincoln, University of Nebraka Press, 2004.

Dennis Townsend Papers, 1833-1858. Dolph Briscoe Center for American History, University of Texas at Austin.

Doble, John. *John Doble's Journal and Letters from the Mines: Mokelumne Hill, Jackson, Volcano and San Francisco, 1851-1865*, Charles L. Camp, ed. Denver, Old West Publishing Company, 1962. Paperback edition by Volcano Press, Inc., 1999 with variant subtitle: *Volcano, Mokelumne Hill*, Jackson and San Francisco.

Mayo, Leslee. "Dennis Townsend: Inventor of the Folding Globe," Townsend Society of America.

Meacham, Bessie. *A Chronicle of the Family of William Townsend, 1780-1865 and Susannah Smith 1783-1820 and Hannah G. Bigelow, 1794-1865: The Story of the Comings and Goings of Fifteen Sons and Daughters*, 1964.

Meacham, Bessie K. *Index to the Townsend Papers: Dennis Townsend*, Vermont, Public Records Division, Montpelier, 1964, microfilm.

Townsend, Dennis, *Townsend's Folding Globe Lessons: Designed Especially for Family Instruction and the Use of Classes in Schools*. Burlington, Vt, Free Press Print, 1870.

Townsend, Francis Torrey. *Autobiography of Francis Torrey Townsend and Genealogy of the Townsends*. reprint White River, Junction, Vt, Cummings the Printer, 1905.

Watson, Jeanne Hamilton, ed. *To the Land of Gold and Wickedness: The 1848-59 Diary of Lorena L. Hays*, St. Louis, The Patrice Press, 1988.

William Townsend Family Letters 1827-1899. Vermont Historical Society.

Secondary Sources

Aspinwall, Janet L. *Golden Prospects: Daguerreotypes of the California Gold Rush*. Hall Family Foundation in Association with the Nelson Atkins Museum of Art, Kansas City, Missouri, 2019.

Braude, Ann. *Radical Spirits: Spiritualism and Women's Rights in Nineteenth Century America*, 2nd edition. Bloomington, IN, Indiana University Press, 1989, 2001.

Bean, Walton E. *California: An Interpretive History*, 2nd edition. Berkeley, University of California, 1973.

Cenotto, Larry. *Logan's Alley: Amador County Yesterdays in Picture and Prose*, 5 vols. Jackson, Cenotto Publications, 1988-2006.

Coburn, Jesse L. *Letters of Gold: California Postal History through 1869*. U.S. Philatelic Classic Society, Inc. 1864.

Daniels, Rudolph. *Trains Across the Continent: North American Railroad History*, 2nd ed. Bloomington and Indianapolis, Indiana University Press, 1997, 2000.

Davis, Gilbert A. *Historical Sketch of Reading, Windsor County, Vermont, and its Inhabitants from the First Settlement of the Town to 1874*. Bellows Falls, Steam Press of A.N. Swain, 1874.

[Dixon, Elsie] *The Shenandoah Valley Area of Amador County, California, 1854-1904*, Sacramento, 1976.

Gamber, Wendy. *The Boardinghouse in Nineteeth-Century America*, Baltimore, The Johns Hopkins, University Press, 2007.

Ho for California! Women's Overland Diaries from the Huntington Library. Edited and annotated by Sandra L. Myres, San Marino, 1980.

Holliday, J.S. *Rush for Riches: Gold Fever and the Making of California*. Oakland Museum of California and the University of California Press, 1999.

Holliday, J.S. *The World Rushed In: the California Gold Rush Experience*. New York, Simon & Schuster, 1981.

Inskeep, Steve. *Imperfect Union: How Jessie and John Fremont Mapped the West, Invented Celebrity, and Helped Cause the Civil War*. New York, Penguin Press, 2020.

Johnson, Susan Lee. *Roaring Camp: The Social World of the California Gold Rush* New York. W.W. Norton & Company, 2000.

Kearnes, Doris Goodwin. *Team of Rivals: The Political Genius of Abraham Lincoln*. New York, Simon & Schuster, 2005.

Kaestle, Carl E. *Pillars of the Republic: Common Schools and American Society 1780-1860*. New York, Hill & Wang, 1983.

Levy, Jo Ann. *They Saw the Elephant: Women in the California Gold Rush*. Norman, University of Oklahoma Press, 1992.

[Mason, Jesse D.] *History of Amador County, California, with Illustrations and Biographical Sketches of its Prominent Men and Pioneers*. Oakland, Thompson and West, 1881.

Maxwell, Anne. *Women Photographers of the Pacific World, 1857-1930*. New York, Routledge, 2020.

McPherson, James M. *Battle Cry of Freedom: the Civil War Era.* New York, Oxford University Press, 1998.

Mattes, Merril J. Platte River Road Narratives. Chicago, University of Illinois Press, 1988.

Morrissey, Charles T. *Vermont: A Bicentennial History.* New York, W.W. Norton & Company, Inc., 1981.

Neem, Johann N. *Democracy's Schools: The Rise of Public Education in America.* Baltimore, John Hopkins University Press, 2017.

Nevins, Alan, *War for the Union: Vol. 1, The Improvised War, 1861-1862.* New York, Konesky & Konesky, 1971.

Rolle, Andrew W. *California: A History*, 6th ed. Wheeling, Ill., Harlan Davidson, Inc., 2003.

Swett, John. *History of the Public School System in California.* San Francisco, A.L. Bancroft, 1876.

Tate, Michael I. *Indians and Emigrants: Encounters on the Overland Trails.* Norman, University of Oklahoma Press, 2006.

Unruh, John D., Jr. *The Plains Across: The Overland Emigration and the Trans-Mississippi West, 1840-1860.* Urbana, University of Illinois Press, 1979.

Weiler, Kathleen. *Country Schoolwomen: Teaching in Rural California, 1850-1950*, Stanford, CA, Stanford University Press, 1998.

Schlissel Lillian. *Women's Diaries of the Westward Journey*, New York, Schocken Books, 2004.

Zimmerman, Jonathan, *Small Wonder: The Little Red Schoolhouse in History and Memory*, New Haven, Yale University Press, 2009.

Zorbas, Elaine. *Banished and Embraced: The Chinese in Fiddletown and the Mother Lode.* Plymouth, Mythos Press, 2015.

Zorbas, Elaine. *Fiddletown: From Gold Rush to Rediscovery.* Altadena, Mythos Press, 1997.

Images of the Globe
https://www.abaa.org/book/244935413

https://archive.org/details/dr_townsends-patent-folding-globe-patent-ed-by-dennis-townsend-feb-16-1869-00084027

https://vermonthistory.org/catalog?search_collection=globe&search=Search&entry=a9ad9700-89a0-11ea-9760-cfd273e2ec6c

https://www.davidrumsey.com/luna/servlet/detail/RUMSEY~8~1~411~80026:Townsend-s-Patent-Folding-Globe

Resources on the Web

http://www.actforlibraries.org/using-the-long-tom-in-gold-mining/

https://www.american-rails.com/1840s.html

https://www.ancestry.com/

https://about.usps.com/news/national-releases/2012/pr12_civil-war-mail-history.pdf

https://about.usps.com/who/profile/history/postmaster-finder/postmasters-by-city.htmn

https://about.usps.com/who/profile/history/overland-mail.htm

https://archive.org/details/scientificamerican1870scie

https://archive.org/details/calteach09unse

https://archive.org/details/dr_promotion-text-for-townsends-patent-folding-globe--publishers-george-00084030

https://www.britannica.com/technology/telegraph

https://etc.usf.edu/maps/pages/3300/3339/3339.htm

https://www.loc.gov/collections/music-of-nineteenth-century-ohio/articles-and-essays/singing-schools

http://www.malakoff.com/goldcountry/capiclet.htm

https://moaningcaverns.com

http://oneroomschoolhousecenter.weebly.com/americas-one-rooms.html

https://octa-trails.org/

https://www.paper-trail.org/

https://www.scientificamerican.com/article/atmospheric-rivers-california-megaflood-lessons-from-forgotten-catastrophe/ Ingram, B. Lynn, *Scientific American*, January 1, 2013

http://www.yosemite.ca.us/library/hutchings_california_magazine

https://www.vtstateparks.com/ascutney.html

https://vermonthistory.org/documents/findaid/townsend.pdf

https://vermonthistory.org/documents/digital/TownsendsFoldingGlobeLessons.pdf

https://vermonthistory.org/documents/findaid/townsend.pdf

https://vermonthistory.org/documents/digital/TownsendsFoldingGlo-
beLessons.pdf

 www.superstitionsof.com/superstitions-of-the-moon.htm.

https://en.wikipedia.org/wiki/Fall_River_Line

https://en.wikipedia.org/wiki/Hannibal_and_St._Joseph_Railroad

https://en.wikipedia.org/wiki/Tavern

Newspapers
    Amador Ledger
    Amador Ledger and Amador Record
    Sacramento Daily Union
    Vermont Chronicle
    Volcano Weekly Ledger

Index

Fiddletown 35, 36, 37, 38, 39, 40, 41, 43, 44, 45, 46, 47, 48, 49, 50, 52, 54, 55, 56, 57, 58, 59, 60, 62, 63, 64, 65, 66, 67, 68, 69, 71, 72, 74, 75, 76, 82, 83, 87, 91, 93, 95, 97, 99, 101, 102, 103, 104, 106, 108, 118, 123, 131, 132, 133, 134, 135, 136, 140, 141, 142
  Cemeteries 136, 142
  Dry Creek 35, 44, 72
  Fiddletown Schoolhouse 44, 45, 82, 88
Fires 90, 91
Florida 84, 119, 142
French 42, 61

G

Gambling 36, 43, 60, 65, 69, 70, 72
Geography 89, 117, 119, 122, 123, 136
Gold Rush 1, 11, 16, 28, 35, 37, 39, 41, 42, 44, 47, 71, 82, 87

H

Hays, Lorena 12, 14, 16, 37, 42
Herrick, Aurelia Townsend 2, 5, 36, 39, 40, 41, 42, 43, 44, 45, 47, 48, 50, 56, 57, 64, 66, 67, 69, 72, 74, 75, 76, 82, 83, 85, 86, 87, 92, 93, 95, 97, 99, 103, 106, 117, 118, 119, 120, 121, 122, 124, 125, 126, 132, 135, 142, 143
Hispanic population 41
Holt, Orlando 53, 57, 60
Homestead Act 82
Hotels
  St. Charles 140, 141, 142
  Veranda 140

I

Illinois 1, 5, 6, 10, 12, 21, 22, 48, 55, 84, 101, 123, 133
  Carrollton 1, 5, 6, 10, 22, 101, 123
Immigrants 41, 82
Indians 3, 12, 13, 14, 22, 26, 37, 54, 60, 61, 65, 82
  Pawnees 14, 26
  Sioux 13, 14, 26
Ione 12, 42, 45, 48, 140, 141
Iowa 4, 13, 22, 26, 73, 86, 92, 121, 124, 131, 142, 143

J

Jackson 4, 17, 18, 45, 70, 82, 88, 89, 97, 133, 134

New York 3, 39, 42, 46, 48, 67, 69, 84, 99, 118, 119, 120

O

Ohio 4, 10, 12, 142

P

Pacific Mail Steamship Company 39, 46, 67, 72, 76, 118
Panama 39, 46, 118
Perry, Jane Ray 40, 41, 56, 58, 64, 141
Perry, Samuel R. 41, 64
Photography 47, 48, 49
  Daguerreotype 18, 48, 60, 69, 74, 83
Placer County 142
  Loomis 141
Placerville 16, 57
Platte River 10, 11, 13, 22, 26

R

Railroads 21, 46, 54, 118, 123, 126, 131
Rancheria Massacre 41, 42, 65, 70
Ray, John 56, 141
Russell, John 22

S

Sacramento 12, 17, 20, 24, 35, 37, 39, 40, 44, 50, 52, 55, 57, 59, 60, 63, 65,
      71, 75, 83, 99, 100, 123, 131, 133, 141
Salt Lake City 11, 14, 15, 16, 22, 27, 28, 46
San Francisco 18, 35, 39, 41, 46, 67, 72, 75, 89, 99, 118
Savage, George 120, 121, 123
Schools 68, 83, 88, 89, 90, 93, 104, 133
Shenandoah Valley 141
Sierra Nevada foothills 11, 16, 35, 38, 46, 131
Singing schools 47, 76, 82, 85
Slavery 5, 67, 83, 84, 85, 86, 91, 92, 101, 108
Smith, Susannah 1, 2, 30, 105, 142
Steamships 39, 46, 76
Stockton State Hospital 133, 134
Sunning. *See* Toishan
Sutter Creek 17, 45, 140
Swain, Oliver 55
Swett, John 89, 92, 93

Wolcott 117, 120, 125
Volcano 10, 11, 12, 16, 17, 18, 19, 22, 24, 25, 26, 35, 36, 38, 40, 43, 45, 48, 52,
    60, 70, 87, 88, 89, 90, 91, 93, 94, 101, 102, 103, 104, 106, 108, 135, 140
  Volcano Schoolhouse 88, 93, 104
Volcano Cut-off 16, 17, 88

W

Waterman, Henry 86, 121
Waterman, Isabelle Townsend 2, 20, 85, 86, 104, 121, 124, 131, 135, 142, 143
Weather 3, 10, 12, 14, 15, 16, 19, 20, 23, 25, 26, 27, 28, 30, 35, 38, 46, 49,
    50, 52, 57, 58, 62, 63, 69, 83, 87, 95, 102, 106, 107, 108, 123, 124, 126,
    131, 136
  Floods 99
Williams, Mary Ann Ray 101, 123
Wisconsin 57, 60
Withington, Elizabeth 48

Y

Young, Brigham 15, 27